New Mexico's

Sanctuaries, Retreats, and Sacred Places

Text and photography by
Christina Nealson

WESTCLIFFE PUBLISHERS

www.westcliffepublishers.com

International Standard Book Number: 1-56579-423-0

Text and photography copyright: Christina Nealson, 2001. All rights reserved.

Editor: Kelly Kordes Anton
Designer: Angie Lee, Grindstone Graphics, Inc.
Production Manager: Craig Keyzer

Published by:
Westcliffe Publishers, Inc.
P.O. Box 1261
Englewood, CO 80150
www.westcliffepublishers.com

Printed in China through: World Print, Ltd.

Library of Congress Cataloging-in-Publication Data:

Nealson, Christina, 1950-
    New Mexico's sanctuaries, retreats, and sacred places / by Christina Nealson.
        p. cm.
    Includes bibliographical references and index.
    ISBN 1-56579-423-0
    1. Sacred space--New Mexico--Guidebooks. 2. Shrines--New Mexico--
Guidebooks. 3. New Mexico--Guidebooks. I. Title.

    BL2527.N6 .N43 2001
    291.3'5'09789--dc21   2001026027

For more information about other fine books and calendars from Westcliffe Publishers, please contact your local bookstore, call us at 1-800-523-3692, write for our free color catalog, or visit us on the Web at **www.westcliffepublishers.com.**

Please Note: *Risk is always a factor in backcountry and high-mountain travel. Many of the activities described in this book can be dangerous, especially when weather is adverse or unpredictable, and when unforeseen events or conditions create a hazardous situation. The author has done her best to provide the reader with accurate information about backcountry travel, as well as to point out some of its potential hazards. It is the responsibility of the users of this guide to learn the necessary skills for safe backcountry travel, and to exercise caution in potentially hazardous areas. The author and publisher disclaim any liability for injury or other damage caused by backcountry traveling or performing any other activity described in this book.*

Cover Photo: The Benedictine monks at the Monastery of Christ in the Desert welcome visitors for the day or a longer stay.

Opposite: The Great Kiva, an Anasazi ruin, is a round, covered ceremonial chamber.

Acknowledgments

This book and I had many helpers. Special thanks to the folks at Westcliffe Publishers, especially Linda Doyle—caring, committed, and forever helpful—who set this ship to sail. Thanks to Jenna Samelson, managing editor at Westcliffe, for her flexibility and support. And finally, thanks to John Fielder for his commitment to this creative, expansive project.

I could not have completed my research without help from the books in the bibliography, as well as conversations with and feedback from friends such as authors Bill deBuys and Susan Tweit. Thanks to the folks at the Las Cruces Archdiocese archives and the Santa Fe Historic Foundation, and archeologists Judy Propper and Tom Cartledge. Thanks to Dave Schumacher for the loan of exceptional books from his private collection. Thanks to my cousin, Deac Cain, who braved Iowa ice and snow to gather information. Thanks to the "keepers of the inns," who met me with a smile and a warm hello, especially Michael and Cathy at La Foresta, Hosen at Bodhi Manda Zen Center, Father Michael at Our Lady of Guadalupe Benedictine Abbey, as well as my hosts at Black River, la Casitas de Gila, Monastery of Christ in the Desert, and Zuni Lodge. And thanks to my friend Stephen Jones, always there, with care.

Thank you, daughter Hope, photographer extraordinaire and sounding board. Blessings and praise to Mom and Dad, who celebrate 60 years of holy continuity. Your "How's the book coming along?" over long-distance lines means more than you'll ever know.

Mil gracias to my best friend and husband, Tom Wolf. His Catholic worship, forestry knowledge, and infinite wisdom permeate the words of this book. His editing clears the clutter and his love and companionship keep my heart light.

Finally, gratitude to sister rattlesnake, guardian of the waters, the primera New Mexico resident of desert, field, and plain. While working on this book, I saw your magnificent, slithering body twice, and I am forever richer for it.

Opposite: This mosaic contributes to the beautiful array of artwork at Our Lady of Guadalupe Benedictine Abbey in Pecos.

Contents

Regional Map of New Mexico 8–9

Preface 10

Introduction 13

How to Use This Guide 15

Visiting Sacred Sites 19

The Nature of New Mexico 23

Glossary of Spiritual Significance 25

Regions of New Mexico

1 **Northwest: Earth that Bedazzles** 34

2 **North Central: The Holy Heart** 58

3 **Northeast: The Windswept Corner** 158

4 **Southeast: The Enchanted Lands** 172

5 **Southwest: The Wild and Woolly Corner** 200

Appendix A: Historical Time Line of New Mexico 242

Appendix B: Schedule of Native American
             Feast Days and Spectacles 246

Appendix C: Retreats by Spiritual Affiliation 249

Appendix D: Bibliography and Suggested Reading List 250

Index 252

About the Author/Photographer 256

Opposite: Church ruins, a reminder of New Mexico's rich spiritual past.

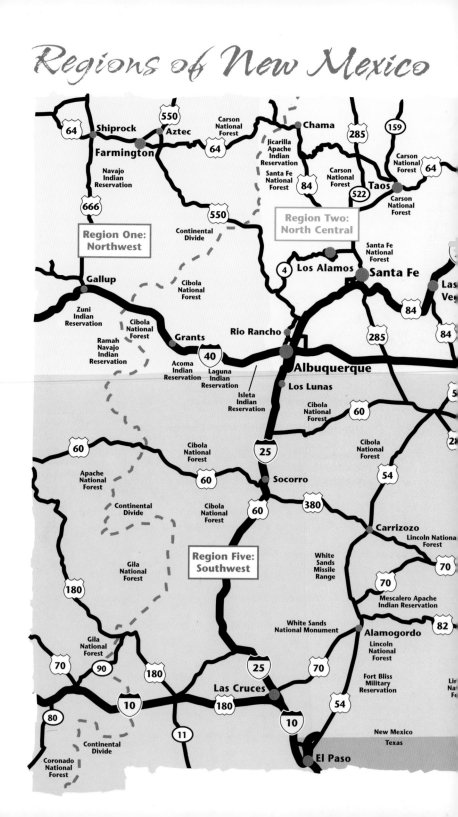

Regions of New Mexico

Raton

N

64
87

56

Kiowa
National
Grasslands

Kiowa
National
Grasslands

39

**Region Three:
Northeast**

54

Tucumcari

40

209

84

60

60
84

Clovis

egion Four:
Southeast

Portales

70

206

380

Roswell

285

82

Artesia

18

62
180

arlsbad
averns
ational
Park

Carlsbad

18

A cross hangs on an adobe wall in the ruins of a church.

Preface

Sig and Inga always seemed old to me. Like grandparents. Even though, in the line of family relations, they were actually my second cousins. To me, growing up on the farmlands of Iowa, they were a precious, dedicated Danish couple who homesteaded 26 acres outside the small town of West Branch. I spent many a day and night with them in their small, white clapboard farmhouse with no indoor plumbing, no television, and a coal furnace that never quite pushed the heat to the tiny upstairs bedroom.

Mornings began at daybreak, when we collected soft, newly hatched eggs from under the toasty bellies of hens. We sat on small, wooden stools and hand-milked the cows, poured the warm milk into the separator, turned the crank, and sent the liquid into two spouts: milk and cream. After a short prayer and a lunch of open-faced sandwiches on homemade bread along with the requisite coffee—*all* Danes drank coffee, even kids— we jumped into their old black Ford to travel across the gravel roads of the rolling countryside. On these pilgrimages, Sig and Inga photographed barns, winding rivers, and the few remaining original prairie patches inside cemetery fences. On these journeys, Sig looked down into the viewfinder of his antique box camera and preserved priceless black-and-white images of the Iowa landscape.

Once home, with evening chores complete, Sig and Inga closed up their tiny kitchen. They plugged in those mysterious red lights and developed the pictures in ceramic trays under the water of a hand pump, with the help of thermometers and hot water from the stove (they had no hot water in their house). To this little girl, it was magic. As I consider it now, their art was nothing short of holy.

Sig and Inga were my greatest teachers of how to do photography. Not so much the technicalities, although they gave me many books and answered my myriad questions on the subject. My greatest lessons actually came from watching them unfold photography into a simple day of passion—an extension of the soul that involved a mysterious countryside journey, the play and prayer of light, and a captured image. They did not travel distant lands to find and record the precious and the beautiful. In their small circle, Iowa barns and cornfields never ceased to enthrall.

My path has been very different from theirs—I've had the privilege to see and photograph distant lands. I shot my collection of barn images in many states, and for more than 20 years I traveled the backcountry throughout the American Southwest, Mexico, Guatemala, Honduras, Nicaragua, and Zimbabwe, photographing women and children, landscapes, wildlife, and ancient ruins. (To see my photos, including images of the Southwest and Zimbabwe, visit my website at www.christinanealson.com)

These many years saw many equipment changes, film changes, and switches to and from black-and-white. Today, my preference is color, and my cameras are two Nikon N90s. My lenses (all Nikon) include a 24–50mm f/3.3–4.5 AF Nikkor, a 70–300mm f/4–5.6 AF Nikkor, a 28–200mm f/3.5–5.6 AF Nikkor, and a 55mm f/2.8 micro-Nikkor. I travel light, with a Tamrac Extreme Series photo backpack and a photographer's vest. As a small woman with tiny hands, I find that this equipment fits me perfectly. For this book, I shot with primarily Fuji Velvia and Sensia 100 film.

Sig passed away earlier this year, released from the clutches of a nursing home and a body that failed his never-ceasing independent spirit. Inga, at 95 years old, will see this book—with great happiness on her part and mine. And if I know Sig, a critique from heaven will be forthcoming. Viva!

This book is for all who seek, that you may find.
It is dedicated to Inga and Signor Larsen, who showed me
how the sacred dwells in the everyday acts of a simple life.

St. Joseph of the Lake Mission Church at the Old Laguna Pueblo.

Introduction

*W*hen Linda Doyle at Westcliffe Publishers contacted me about this book, it was as if a gift dropped out of the heavens. After 10 years in the Sangre de Cristo Mountains of Colorado—16 miles from the nearest small town—I had recently moved to Taos, N.M. Previously, I left my professional and personal roles behind in Boulder, Colo., and moved into the Sangre de Cristo mountain wilderness on 40 acres of designated "wasteland." (In the middle of nowhere, with "nothing" but piñon trees and views for hundreds of miles? It was perfect!) In southern Colorado, I spent more than half my time in solitary spiritual journey.

There, I dreamed, schemed, and built a small, seven-sided cabin, and lived alone. I listened to the language of the trees and the wind, the wisdom of seasonal cycles, and—for the first time in my life—unearthed my own true rhythms, free of other people's expectations. No longer consumed by the roles of mother (my daughter had left for college), wife, or psychotherapist, I protected my solitude with fierce boundaries, as I dug my little spring for water, adjusted two solar panels, and emptied the composting toilet. On my precious land, named Dancing Raven, I lived simply and quietly, with my Old English sheepdog, horse, and two cats. And I wrote every day.

After several years, I joined my new life-partner, Tom Wolf, a writer, naturalist, and fan of that great American philosopher, Donald Duck. Seems while I was writing away in my tiny log-and-glass cabin on the west face of the Sangres, Tom was doing the same on the east face, over the Sangres' 13,000-foot spine. We lived together, tucked away in the Sangres, for another four years before we moved out of forested solitude and into a town that met our artistic and spiritual needs. The place, Taos, touched our beloved Sangre de Cristo Mountains, so in this most important sense, we never left home.

I was settled in Taos when Westcliffe presented this book opportunity to me. Although I'd traveled and hiked throughout New Mexico for 20 years, now it was my home. So, I was more than excited to create a book with the purpose of leading people to special places on behalf of spirit. I was exceedingly flattered to have publisher John Fielder not only validate my writing, but give me the go-ahead to provide the photos. I am honored to unite my work as author and photographer for this very special purpose.

Opposite: Mountaintop shrines like this one are a testament to people's spiritual expression.

New Mexico presents you with many reasons to consider it for your spiritual excursion. You've undoubtedly heard people describe the powerful beauty of the light. There literally is magic in the air. And there is nothing like the convergence of the smell of burning piñon and the deep pounding of the drum at a pueblo. Without doubt, the power of many of New Mexico's special places differs greatly from that in other parts of the United States.

To understand why, it's important to know a little history of New Mexico. For thousands of years, various Indian groups inhabited these lands. The heirs of these people continue to live here, many in pueblos and lands set aside as sovereign Native American nations. While most of the United States looks east for its post-1500 settlement history, New Mexico looks primarily south, to Mexico, and ultimately to Spain and even to the Moors.

As a result of its history, New Mexico is home to an unusual combination of sanctuaries, retreats, sacred places, and events—all of which captured my enthusiasm and imagination for this book. Stunningly beautiful adobe sanctuaries, hundreds of years old, flourish in the New Mexico terrain, and the landscape is festooned with sacred places confirmed over and over again through Native American mythology and Hispanic story. These retreats lie gently upon the earth, providing solace to the modern, often-weary spirit. And as you will see, as I set out on my journeys, it became inevitable for me to include a sampling of the myriad spiritual events that take place throughout the four seasonal cycles. From Pueblo Indian Feast Days, to the arduous pilgrimages to Our Lady of Guadalupe, to the mass ascension of thousands of geese and cranes, this magnificent state brims with events in which you can participate and breathe the holy.

In today's whizzing, whirling world, we need to know where to go to find silence and to access those deeper voices within and outside of ourselves. Not everyone can do what I did, retreating into the mountains for many years. But you can get in your car, open the windows to the crystalline air with its scent of sage, and steer your way to special places of peace and power. Sanctuaries that embrace and protect. Retreats of renewal. Places where you can hear your soul speak. Events of spectacle that stop you in your tracks and lift you into a holy realm.

As you journey with this book, may you be moved to tears as you meet the magnificent landscape, wildlife, and people of these extraordinary places. Tears of humbleness, sadness, ecstasy, joy, fear, and jubilation. As you cross vast, sparse deserts, ascend holy mountains, walk deep, rocky canyons, and wade broad and narrow waters. Into sacred, ancient Indian ruins. Hauntingly beautiful shrines. Thick and powerful earthen walls adorned with colorful religious carvings, crosses, crucifixes, and handwritten prayers—all to the whisper of the wind, the jingle of bells, the shake of a rattle.

May your tears fall long and softly, as imagination sparks, spirit meets place, and soul whispers hope. For spiritual renewal, there's simply no other place like New Mexico.

Cerro Pedernal (Flint Peak) has served as a physical and spiritual sentinel for centuries.

How to Use This Guide

In writing this book, I tried my darndest to give you a healthy head start into a wide variety of sites and enough information to determine if a place fits your needs and expectations. I steadfastly believe that the heart of a spiritual journey lies in the ability to create a space where the unexpected dream or revelation can drop in. Where you can hear the soul speak. It is, really, as much about the unplanned as the planned. This book walks that fine line, giving you a place to start and plan, but providing sites with the potential to raise you out of the ordinary and into the sublime.

Regional Designations and Maps

To help you navigate this book, I divided the state of New Mexico into five geographic regions: Northwest, North Central, Northeast, Southeast, and Southwest. The regions each have their own chapter which includes a short, introductory description of the area along with a map.

Each region's chapter includes four primary sections—Sanctuaries, Retreats, Sacred Places, and Spiritual Events—along with short lists of other sites and events I found too interesting to ignore. Although it's somewhat hard to classify these destinations, I considered "sanctuaries" places you can visit for the day and "retreats" places for overnight visits. "Sacred places" are natural, outdoor settings, while "spiritual events" are scheduled events such as feast days and pilgrimages. If you're planning a spiritual journey within a specific geographic region, numbers on the regional maps at the beginning of each chapter indicate the location of each site.

Site Listings

Within each region and each section, the sites are listed alphabetically. Each site has a corresponding numerical mark on its respective regional map to help you to orient yourself to the location and to indicate its proximity to other sites you may want to experience. In the Sanctuaries, Retreats, and Sacred Places sections, each site description begins with a bulleted list to quickly present you with pertinent information:

Location: Tells you where the site is.

Description: Tells you what the site is like—whether it's a formal retreat center, trail, church, etc.

Spiritual Significance: Lists the attributes of the place (except retreats) that have spiritual power, such as kiva, ruins, and streams, all of which are discussed in the Glossary of Spiritual Significance, page 25. This glossary defines terms, many rooted in Native American beliefs and Spanish/Mexican conquests, and laced with a strong dose of Catholicism. Any time you run across an unfamiliar term, check the glossary for clarification.

Solitude Rating: A five-star rating system that indicates the site's capacity for solitude. One star means, "Be surprised if you find any," while five stars means, "Here you will find deep, uninterrupted solitude, with little or no effort." Three stars means, "Solitude is possible, but you must make the effort to find or create it." Solitude is relative, of course. And you are most likely to find it early in the morning, late in the day, or off-season (late autumn through early spring). When applicable, I also mention it if a place is dark at night, as I believe darkness is as important as quiet to the spiritual-seeker.

How to get there: Provides detailed instructions that take you to the site.

Accessibility from highway: When applicable, the listings include information about how easy it is to access the site from a major highway.

Facilities: Lists conveniences available at the site, such as food, water, restrooms, and visitor centers.

Fee Area: Tells you whether or not there is a fee to enter and use the area, although the specific dollar amounts are not listed as they can change. Not included for retreats.

Contact Information

For most of the sites in this book, I was able to include a complete address, a phone number, and even a website. But for some places, this was simply not possible, as parts of New Mexico are refreshingly undeveloped. If I discovered a site and was moved by it, I included it, despite a lack of backup information. The raw nature of New Mexico is a large part of its charm and potency. You will find, as you venture forth, it teaches humility.

Appendices

To help you learn about the events that deeply shape the spiritual land-scape and psyche of New Mexico, I provide several helpful appendices at the back of this book. I strongly encourage you to read both the Glossary of Spiritual Significance (page 25) and Appendix A (page 242) before you begin any spiritual journeys.

Appendix A: Historical Time Line of New Mexico. Provides a short time line of major historical events.

Appendix B: Schedule of Native American Feast Days and Spectacles. Offers a month-by-month summary of Native American spiritual celebrations, for planning purposes.

Appendix C: Retreats by Spiritual Affiliation. Lists the retreats according to their spiritual orientation, for easy reference.

Appendix D: Bibliography and Suggested Reading List. Suggests books to accompany you on your spiritual sojourn, plus lists the books I drew upon for factual reference. (If I had to choose one book for you to read, it would be Willa Cather's *Death Comes for the Archbishop*...then again, there's D.H. Lawrence.)

Visiting Sacred Sites

I'm all for a spontaneous, go-where-your-heart-takes-you journey—but it helps to be prepared. Skim through this book and choose the places, retreats, and events that appeal to you. Then, pack appropriately, bringing just what you need, and leaving excess baggage (both physically and metaphorically) behind. Finally, it's important to know how to behave while discovering these sacred lands.

Choose a Site

You'd hate to drive miles and miles to a retreat to find the campground full or a place closed. The first rule of embarking on a spiritual journey in New Mexico is to *call first!* Here, on seemingly ordinary days, even places operated by the federal government are closed for special Native American ceremonies. And Native American pueblos can be closed for various reasons. For spiritual events, call ahead, as offices are commonly closed on the event day.

The religious, nonprofit retreats in this book are priced at $55 a night or less and include meals, while the secular, privately owned listings are on the higher end. For up-to-date prices and meal information, call or check a listing's website. When places do not have modern conveniences, I mention it. Most of the retreats in this book have electricity, but a few are run by solar power. Having lived for several years without power lines, I can tell you that a special calm comes from the absence of electromagnetic interference. When I find a retreat with this opportunity, I say so. Likewise, when I find a retreat that offers night skies and darkness, I say so.

So, beyond price and availability, what do you ask of a place you are considering for retreat? I suggest the following:

- How far is the retreat from the nearest town?
- Does your facility have special, daily events for retreatants, or does it offer a solely unstructured retreat?
- What special accommodations do you offer for a solitary retreatant?
- Is there spiritual counseling and guidance available at this facility?
- Is your facility dark at night?
- Are there places to walk and hike?

Opposite: The Bodhi Manda Zen Center in Jemez Springs is a quiet retreat by a rambling river.

- How many meals do you serve a day? (All the places I visited that serve meals also accommodate special dietary restrictions.)
- Are there phones and televisions in the rooms? (For most places in this book, the answer is no.)
- Do you allow cell phones? Is their use controlled?
- Do you allow dogs or children?

What to Bring

While packing clothing and supplies, the most important thing to keep in mind is to be prepared for weather extremes and changes. Temperatures can shoot up to 113 degrees in the desert, and it can snow in July in the mountains. Pack and wear layers of clothes, so you can add and shed items as the temperature changes. I highly recommend rain pants and a rain jacket—some of the most awesome experiences happen in the rain, when you are the only one out and about. Thick-soled shoes with good traction are a must, preferably with leather uppers to guard against cactus spines and snakes (yes, snakes). And don't forget your swimsuit, flashlight, insect repellent, hat, binoculars, drinking water, sandals, and a good map. (I recommend the *New Mexico Road & Recreation Atlas* published by Benchmark Maps, widely available at stores in New Mexico, or call 800-962-1394.) The sun can be excruciatingly hot—especially on feast-day dances—so be sure to bring sunglasses, sunscreen, a wide-brimmed hat, and maybe even an umbrella. If you're attending spiritual events, bring a collapsible cloth chair (the kind that fits into its own carrying case). At less than $10 from discount stores, they're great for sitting down to watch pueblo dances or to just admire a beautiful place.

Depending on the destination, purpose, and depth of your retreat, I urge you to take a few things with you for pampering and pleasure. A beautiful, perhaps new, journal and your favorite writing pen. (Beware: a change of altitude often causes fountain pens to leak.) Bring art supplies for painting or drawing, your preferred shampoo and bubble bath, a bottle of your favorite wine or liqueur (where allowed), a candle and matches, a photo…and a special book, perhaps (see Appendix D: Bibliography and Suggested Reading List).

What to Leave at Home

The majority of places in this book do not allow dogs, and most of the retreats do not allow either children or dogs. The reason is obvious: these places encourage solitude and watchable wildlife. Both children and dogs are disruptive by nature, bless their hearts, not to mention the sometimes angry and harried adults who attempt to control them. If a place does allow children and/or dogs, you need to determine if this is the level of retreat you seek.

A modern convenience that has an effect on solitude is the use of cell phones. Ask each retreat about their guidelines regarding cell phone use. Please, when visiting a site, event, or retreat, leave your cell phone in the car with the ringer turned off.

We all know the weight of excess baggage, and we have plenty of it in our lives. So when it comes to packing, choose carefully. Travel lightly and wisely. And remember, those roles you take along—spouse, parent, child, caregiver, professional—can carry the weight of a lifetime.

How to Behave

No matter which sanctuary, retreat, sacred place, or spiritual event you decide to attend, a little advice about how to respect the land and the people will make your visit more comfortable—for both you and the people you encounter. Lumped under the heading of "pueblo etiquette," keep the following in mind:

- Pueblos are people's homes. Don't wander into houses unless invited.
- Create absolutely no photos, recordings, or sketches during tribal dances without permission (photo permits and fees vary among pueblos).
- Tribal dances are religious ceremonies, not performances like pow-wows. It is a privilege to witness a ceremony. Keep quiet and don't applaud or touch the dancers. Do not walk across the dance plaza.
- Do not enter kivas or other restricted areas.
- Leave your cell phone in your car.
- Do not bring alcohol or drugs onto pueblo lands.
- Check with each pueblo on their visitor policy, calling first to ensure entry.
- If you plan to attend a feast day or other ceremony, call before the day of the event as they rarely answer phones on ceremonial days.
- Pueblos usually charge you a fee to visit on regular days, but not on feast days. However, it's good to leave a contribution or gift in the church or on the altar near the dancers. Ask permission for entry.
- To enter a shrine, ask permission, then ask if it's appropriate to leave a gift (usually cash or tobacco) and where you might leave it. Each place is different.

The Nature of New Mexico

In New Mexico, you simply must be able to witness many things without knowing the whole story. There are as many, if not more, fictions and fables as there are factual truths—it's enough to make the imagination soar. This is never so true as when you experience a dance or celebration at a pueblo, where asking for explanation is considered rude. While there is hard research in this book, most importantly, I offer the stories of the people who live here, based on their personal experiences.

To grasp an understanding of New Mexico's people, wildlife, and landscape, one thing you must know about is the five-letter word: *water.* Every settlement arisen from the dirt, every dance danced, every trail etched across the landscape, every crop picked, every breath taken…has depended on rain, river, lake, or spring. In this land of dry heat and dry cold, water is sacred.

What about other idiosyncrasies of New Mexico? Well, there's the roadside trash. You will, no doubt, see some and probably find it offensive. I felt the same way when I first moved here. And while it's true I wish the trash weren't here, I've come to appreciate the trade-off. I'll take New Mexico's undeveloped, country ambience any day over a developed, spic-and-span, sparkling-clean landscape, where guardrails block views, chain-link fences protect me from myself and keep me from many spectacular places, and security lights obscure the night sky.

No, New Mexico's ways aren't always proper, paved, and protected, but we are richer for it. Closer to the heartbeat. Nearer to that raw, down-home edge that keeps authenticity in the open. Just north, in Colorado, the highway department takes down *descansos* that dot the highways. Here in New Mexico, these roadside crosses and shrines, thoughtfully placed where a person died in an accident, are considered sacred places. As a Penitente *hermano* (a member of the Penitente Brotherhood, a devout religious order) explained one day, a *descanso* marks a place where the soul has prematurely spilled over. Here, *descansos* are protected and cared for.

This book contains the tame and the wild. The pure and the muddied. The dark and the light. Take your time as you travel across this awe-inspiring landscape, where *descansos* mark death and Penitente *moradas* (churches, meeting houses) hearken the solitary faith of early, remote settlers. Drop your pace to a saunter, the walk of pilgrimage. These pages are just the beginning. The real riches lie in the unwritten words.

Opposite: Taos' Vallecitos Mountain Refuge, designed for public and nonprofit workers, provides a fitting venue for spiritual reconnection.

Glossary of Spiritual Significance

To attempt to define sacred and spiritual significance is, indeed, traipsing a slippery slope. Sacredness is a deeply personal interpretation and opinions are varied and wide. While visiting with three different Navajo people about the origin of red coral in their culture, I heard three different stories. And so it is. Please take these suggestions of spiritual significance not as the one truth, but as one of many interpretations.

As for the sacred places mentioned in this book, remember that Native American sacred sites are often related to tribal creation stories and other significant past events. The sites may be mountains, gathering places of sacred plants, structures, carvings, or burial sites. Often closely connected to religious ceremonies such as vision quests and dances, the sites and the places are inextricably woven together.

Bultos: Three-dimensional carvings. When depicting saints, they are called *santos*. Originally carved from cottonwood root, covered with gesso, and painted.

Cave: The great natural womb of the Mother Earth, sacred places of religious rites, used as healing chambers in times of old. Jesus' crucified body was entombed in a cave, the place of the Resurrection three days later. Caves, such as Aladdin's cave, are also considered places of magic. Abraham was born in a magical cave. People seeking solitude and insight have commonly retreated to caves and deserts. (**Note:** Caves are fragile and often dangerous environments, so please exercise caution when visiting them.)

Confluence, river: The place where two or three rivers or streams meet and flow together. Rivers carry the energies of the landscapes through which they flow, making these very powerful places. A confluence is the meeting place of these energies.

Cristo: Spanish for crucifix; translates to "the Christ" in English.

Crucifix: A cross that includes the image of Christ.

Descanso: Translates to "resting place" in English. Originally, the resting places for the casket bearers on the walk to the *campo santo* (cemetery), the term is now most commonly used for a roadside shrine placed near the site where someone met an untimely death. Usually includes a cross or crucifix, with the name of the deceased and the date of death. It is common in New Mexico to see highly entertaining and colorful representations in memory of the deceased.

Opposite: A fine example of a bulto at Holy Cross Retreat in Mesilla Park.

The term *descanso,* now indicative of a roadside shrine, originally referred to resting places for casket bearers.

Dineh: Translates to "the people," this is the name the Navajo Indians prefer to use. The Spanish actually gave the people the name of "Navajo."

Douglas fir: Often straight and mighty in stature, this is the tree the Tewa climbed to emerge from the lake of their beginning. It is an evergreen, considered a symbol of immortality (see Tree, page 31).

El Camino Real: Originally called *El Camino Real de Tierra Adentro,* "the Royal Road to the Interior," it was the major exploration and trade route from Mexico to the United States, extending from Veracruz on Mexico's east coast, through Mexico City, north to Santa Fe, and eventually to Taos, N.M. Originally following ancient Indian footpaths between North America and Mesoamerica, the caravans on the Camino extended for up to 4 miles, and traveled 5 to 6 miles per day. Eventually the road extended to Taos and beyond.

Farolitos: Translates to "little lanterns" in English. Paper sacks are filled with sand and candles and used as decorations throughout New Mexico during the Christmas season. Lit at dusk on Christmas Eve and allowed to burn through the night, they serve as a symbolic gesture, lighting the way to a shelter for Mary and Joseph. They are generally referred to as *farolitos* by those living north of Interstate 40, and *luminarias* by those south of Interstate 40.

Geoglyphs: Images formed on the ground in what is the most fragile type of rock art. Usually, the surface area is scraped away to form an image in the exposed soil, or a design is arranged on top of the soil with stones.

Hills: In Tewa mythology, the four sacred hills are located between the village and their four sacred mountains. Often the sites of shrines, they are endowed with supernatural spirits.

Ions: An atom or group of atoms that have gained or lost electrons. An atom that loses an electron becomes a positively charged ion. An atom that gains an electron becomes a negatively charged ion. Positive ions, found in occurrences such as warm Chinook (downslope) winds, have predominantly detrimental affects on the body, making one depressed, slow, or irritable. Negative ions, produced by waterfalls, springs, rivers, forests, storms, crashing waves, rock, and the uranium-rich earth of the southwest, produce a calm, soothing, sometimes-transcendental effect. Research indicates that negative ions deregulate the flow of serotonin, a neurotransmitter, to the brain, making serene states and higher consciousness possible. Negative ion fields, also known as "power spots," are abundant at sacred sites.

Kiva: A round, covered ceremonial chamber built into the earth, accessible by ladders or stairs. Considered sacred to the Pueblo Indians and their ancestors. For many, considered the womb of the Mother Earth.

Labyrinth: An intricate, circular structure of interconnecting passages. When used for spiritual purposes in meditation, prayer, or contemplative problem-solving, the path to the center of the soul. Native American and traditional religious leaders alike consider the circle as a spiritual sign of completeness. Labyrinths were commonly painted or inlaid on the floors of medieval cathedrals and churches throughout Europe, with the purpose of *solvitur ambulando,* "to solve by walking."

Lake: Sacred place of the Pueblo peoples, believed to be where the first people emerged. Lakes are often believed to be full of spirits of godlike beings who choose to stay below (see Water, page 32). Powerful Tewa deity spirits are believed to dwell in the lakes located near their four sacred mountains.

Luminarias: Small fires, commonly lit along roadways on Christmas Eve and during pageants in the Christmas season (see Farolitos, page 26).

Marian shrine: A shrine dedicated to one of the many faces of the Virgin Mary, including our Lady of Lourdes, Our Lady of Guadalupe, and Our Lady of Conquistadora. The Goddess/Virgin Mary has many personifications.

Miracle: A supernatural event that defies natural law and has no human explanation. An extraordinary event, wrought by God.

Monastery: A man-made place of retreat, intended to enable people to meet God in silence.

Morada: Chapter house and holy home of Penitente Brotherhoods, consisting of two primary areas: an *oratorio* (chapel room) and living quarters (see Penitentes, page 28).

A geoglyph along La Vista Verde Trail near the Rio Grande Gorge.

Mountain: The breasts of the Great Mother of the universe. Mountain Mother is the source of life-giving water, the rivers of life. The mountains of the

Square Kiva at El Morro National Monument.

Southwest are fecund, lush ecosystems that rise like islands of plenty from the surrounding arid lands. They are the source of medicinal plants, water, food, and game, and are believed sacred because they are endowed with bodies of water.

Mountaintop: In Pueblo mythology, mountaintops are the resting-places of the male God-spirits that inhabit the sky. (The earth was considered female, the sky male.) In Tewa mythology, the top of each mountain is described as the *nan sipu* or "earth navel." The Pueblo plaza is considered the navel of all navels (see Shrine, page 31, and Plaza, page 29). Mountain earth navels—direct paths that lead into the center of the earth—are a gathering place of blessings from all around and are directed inward to the village. The *nan sipu* is held to be one of the rare places where the spirits of Above, Below, and Middle have contact with one another and are accessible to the minds of humans. Mountains also bring people closest to clouds and rainfall, which are precious and most sacred. It is believed by some that supernatural beings dwell at the earth navels on top of the four sacred hills and four sacred mountains of the east, west, north, and south.

Penitentes, Brotherhood of: Devout religious order of New Mexico, based upon fervent rites of penance from 13th-century Europe. Believing it better to suffer in this life than the next, the Penitentes practiced self-flagellation to atone for their sins. They are especially known for their reenactment of the biblical crucifixion on Good Friday, during which many claim they staked a devout follower's hands and feet to a cross. Their communal societies were all-encompassing, providing health care, welfare, and a judicial system. Today's Penitentes, now recognized by the Catholic Church, are few in number and maintain great secrecy. The extreme self-flagellation has been discontinued, and in a few cases, their ceremonies are open to the public.

Petroglyph: Designs scratched into rock using a hard stone. Sacred to today's Native American people, descendants of the artists.

The Penitente brothers of New Mexico gather at *moradas* like this one to practice their longstanding rituals.

Pictograph: Design painted with mineral or vegetable matter and applied by finger, with a yucca fiber brush, or blown through a hollow reed over a mold (as in the case of handprints). Sacred to the Pueblo people, as their ancestors are the artists.

Piñon pine: The state tree of New Mexico, this slow-growing, often-rotund pine dominates the lower altitudes. Evergreen is considered a symbol of immortality and you will see pine boughs in various Native American rituals, sometimes worn in the belt. The long-lasting piñon wood, full of aromatic sap, burns with a nonsparking, orange flame and is valued for firewood and its pungent aroma and warmth. The piñon nut is a favorite, tasty, healthy treat. Piñon pitch has long been used to caulk and patch, to waterproof baskets, and to dye wool (see Tree, page 31).

Plaza: The village center. Large, unpaved areas within Indian pueblos are called "dance plazas," where ritual dances and performances take place. In Tewa tradition, the south plaza, where all dances are initiated, is considered the sacred center of the village. "Plaza" is also the name retained from frontier days, when towns were built defensively to protect Spanish settlers against Indian raids. Village buildings, including homes, a church, stores, and a *torreón,* a defensive tower, were built in a contiguous rectangle, creating an interior plaza with a single entrance. All doors and windows opened to the inside, onto the plaza. When under attack, livestock was herded into the plaza, the sole entrance was secured, and people sought protection in the torreón. Today's most colorful plazas include those of Mesilla, Lincoln, Santa Fe, and Taos, as well as Chimayo's Plaza del Cerro.

Petroglyph at Three Rivers Petroglyphs site north of Alamogordo.

Pueblo: The sacred, ancient home of Pueblo Indians. Each is its own sovereign nation with its own distinct culture and particular set of laws.

Pueblo etiquette: The way you should behave while visiting a pueblo or other site mentioned in this book (see How to Behave, page 21).

Pueblo Revolt of 1680: One of the most significant and defining events of New Mexico history—the Pueblo, Navajo, and Apache responded to decades of Spanish mistreatment and subjugation of their native spirituality and ways of life. Instigated by Popay, a medicine man from the Pueblo of San Juan, Indian villagers rose up in rebellion. Across the New Mexico territory at least 380 Spanish settlers and all 21 Franciscan friars were killed. Although the Spanish returned and reconquered a dozen years later, the Pueblo Revolt led to new reforms, tolerance for Pueblo customs and beliefs, and large land grants that became the present-day, sovereign Native American homelands for 19 pueblos of New Mexico, Ysleta del Sur, the Hopi, Navajo, Mescalero Apaches, and Jicarilla Apaches.

Reredos: A painted altar screen, often composed of a large cluster of *retablos* (several wooden panels, depicting religious scenes). An expression of Catholic faith, usually Spanish/Hispanic in origin.

Retablo: Painted scenes on wood, originally pine, but today commonly done on other woods or tin. An expression of Catholic faith, usually Spanish/Hispanic in origin.

Retreat: Time apart from the busy, everyday world, for silence and solitude.

River: Flowing water is sacred, whether in rivers, springs, or irrigation ditches. Rivers were traditionally considered the flowing blood and lifeline of the Great Mother Earth. From the Ganges in India, whose waters are believed to make one identical to God, to the Jordan in the Mideast, which is said to remake one's flesh into a child, rivers are believed to have magical, sacred powers. Hence, baptism in rivers is symbolic of the return to the Spirit's birth fluid, rendering one "born again."

Rock: In many belief systems, rocks are alive and contain the wisdom of the universe.

Ruins: The remains of olden Indian cultures, held sacred by today's Native American peoples as places where the spirits of their ancestors continue to dwell.

Santo: Spanish for "saint." Term used for a carved or painted object portraying a holy person, including God, angels, or saints.

Shrine: A container or receptacle for sacred relics; a tomb of a saint or other venerated person; or a site made sacred by a venerated object, prayer, or intent. In pueblo life, often a place of spiritual significance, marked by a stone or a pile of stones, on the periphery of villages, in villages, or on mountaintops (see Mountaintop, page 28).

Springs, wells, and fountains: The place where water rises from the ground is considered sacred, where spirits rise from the underworld and communicate. Considered holy places of worship, they were believed to be passages to earth's womb. In past times, any upsurge of water from the earth was called a fountain, considered the source of the life force. To the Pueblo Indians, any origin of water is considered sacred and a source of life (see Ions, page 26).

Our Lady of Guadalupe looks over the Rio Grande south of Taos.

Tewas: The Indians of the San Juan, Santa Clara, San Ildefonso, and Tesuque Pueblos.

Tiwas (Northern): The Indians of the Taos and Picuris Pueblos.

Tiwas (Southern): The Indians of the Sandía and Isleta Pueblos.

Towas: The Indians of the present-day Jemez Pueblo and the abandoned Pecos Pueblo.

Tree: Considered a sacred gift of nature, a tree can provide medicine, shelter, tools, weapons, shade and protection from summer sun, fuel for winter fires, and beauty. Trees were considered living entities with conscious spirits and different kinds of trees are invested with different powers. In some Pueblo Indian mythology, spruce and pine trees are invested with the power to bring rain and heighten fertility.

Volcano: The word "volcano" comes from the Roman god Vulcan, a great forger and metalworker. His forges lay under the sacred Mount Vesuvius and Mount Etna. Vulcan made thunderbolts and other powerful weapons of the gods. Human beings have long worshipped volcanoes as the source of life, believing that their cauldrons contained eternal fire and regenerated the dead.

Water: Mother of all things, source of all life, the place where life began. One of four sacred elements with air, earth, and fire. In some Pueblo cultures, *kachinas* (deified ancestral spirits) control the rain, while serpents guard the pools. Almost every Native American ritual in New Mexico contains some form of a prayer for water, the necessary ingredient for growth and survival.

Waterfall: Considered by many to be a sacred healing place and generator of negative ions (see Ions, page 26).

Carved or painted objects portraying holy beings, including God, angels, or saints, are called *santos*.

Opposite: A shrine at La Capilla de San Ysidro Labrador in Santa Fe.

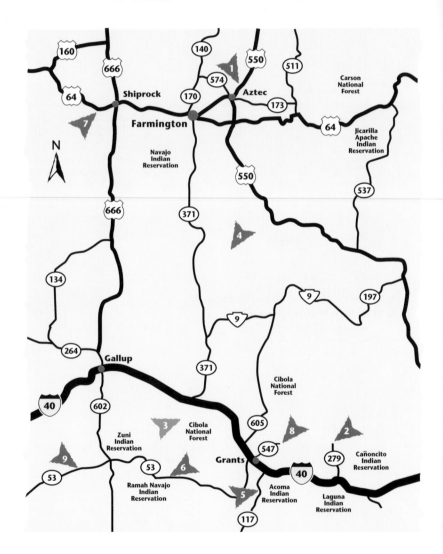

160

666

140

550

511

574

64

Shiprock

170

Aztec

173

Carson
National
Forest

1

7

Farmington

64

Jicarilla
Apache
Indian
Reservation

N

Navajo
Indian
Reservation

550

666

371

537

4

134

9

197

9

264

371

Gallup

Cibola
National
Forest

40

602

3

Cibola
National
Forest

605

8

2

Zuni
Indian
Reservation

547

279

Cañoncito
Indian
Reservation

9

53

6

Grants

5

40

53

Ramah Navajo
Indian
Reservation

Acoma
Indian
Reservation

Laguna
Indian
Reservation

117

*N*early 75 percent of New Mexico's Native American population lives in this stunningly stark and beautiful part of the state. These arid lands of spectacular rock and mesa hold the secrets of ancient times, from the ancestral peoples of Chaco Canyon to today's Jicarilla Apache and from the people of the Acoma, Laguna, and Zuni pueblos to the Navajo (Dineh). Here, myth and landscape combine to stretch the imagination in wondrous directions. Whether you walk the black lava beds of El Malpais or the sacred mountain of Tsoodzil, and whether you stare in wonder at the Rock with Wings or the paradoxes of Chaco Canyon, this region summons your capacity to face the unknown. Austere, dry, and hot, it truly amazes as you ponder the questions of survival and spirit.

Sanctuaries

1. Aztec Ruins, The Great Kiva .... page 36
2. Los Portales Shrine 39
Other Sanctuaries 41

Retreats

3. Zuni Mountain Lodge 42
Other Retreats 43

Sacred Places

4. Chaco Canyon, Supernova Pictograph 44
5. El Malpais National Monument,
     Sandstone Bluffs Overlook 48
6. El Morro National Monument 50
7. Rock with Wings (Tsé Bit' A'í) 52
8. Tsoodzil (Mt. Taylor) 54

Spiritual Events

9. Shalako Dance 56
Other Spiritual Events 56

Sanctuaries

1. Aztec Ruins, The Great Kiva

Aztec Ruins National Monument
84 County Road 2900
Aztec, NM 87410
505-334-6174
www.nps.gov/azru

Location: In the heart of Aztec.

Description: A fully restored ceremonial kiva set within a 12th-century Anasazi pueblo, considered to be one of the largest and best preserved in the country.

Spiritual Significance: Kiva, ruins, stream.

Solitude Rating: ★★

How to get there: The Aztec Ruins are northwest of the city of Aztec, 0.5 mile north of US 550. Follow the signs to the Aztec Ruins National Monument.

Accessibility from highway: Easy.

Facilities: Located in the town of Aztec, everything is close by. Visitor center and picnic area within the ruins site.

Fee Area: Yes.

I first saw this kiva more than 10 years ago, after I visited the awesome keyhole kiva of Casa Rinconada in Chaco Canyon. I spent many quiet hours in Casa Rinconada. Today, you cannot go inside the kiva at Casa Rinconada, but you can enter and sit within the confines of The Great Kiva, at the ruins known as the Place by Flowing Waters. The grandeur of the Aztec Ruins Great Kiva struck deeply, appealing to me in a different way. By the way, the ruins are not, and never have been, Aztec. They are Anasazi. The Aztec culture of central Mexico arose several centuries after this community. When Anglo settlers first came upon these ruins, they mistakenly thought the Aztecs built the pueblos and named the site accordingly.

The Place by Flowing Waters ruins, considered a Chaco outlier, is 55 miles north of Chaco Canyon. Completed just before Chaco was fully abandoned, a major 30-foot-wide road linked the two communities. The only Anasazi site larger than these ruins is Pueblo Bonito in Chaco Canyon.

This kiva, 45 feet in diameter, was excavated by Earl Morris in 1921 and reconstructed 13 years later. The kiva's original roof was a miracle in itself, covering 1,832 square feet with wood and dirt a foot thick. The original roof would have weighed 95 tons, the supporting limestone disks quarried from mountains at least 40 miles away. People now believe the restored roof is higher than the original, but the rest of what you see and feel is as close to authentic as it can be.

Just what went on in this Great Kiva remains a mystery. It was most definitely used for ceremonies and detailed rituals that renewed people's connection with the sky and earth, sun and moon, winter and summer. To enter a kiva is to enter the earth's womb and reconnect with our spiritual and mythic origins in the underworld, with spirits past and present. To further add to the mystery, this kiva is built on the same meridian line—a 700-km line that continues southward to the great ruins of Casa Grandes in Mexico—as Casa Rinconada in Chaco Canyon. Some theorize that the people moved here from Chaco and then traveled south and built Casa Grandes. Stories of the Laguna and Acoma confirm the ancient ones' great travels to the north and south.

The people who lived here marked the times for planting, harvesting, and holding ceremonies by the movement of the sun, moon, and stars. Select individuals observed the sun on the horizon each morning. To these people, who had no word for "religion," all places where the earth and sky touched were sacred. Their Great Kiva may have served as a gathering point to acknowledge and connect with the great mysteries.

Sit quietly and hear the distant drum as the summer-solstice sun slices its way through the opening, signaling, informing, setting human spirit into motion with prayers of thanksgiving and renewal in the Place by Flowing Waters.

2. Los Portales Shrine

Seboyeta (Cebolleta)

$\mathcal{S}$eboyeta is a small, sleepy village. We are their guests, so please honor their slow pace and peaceful quiet. To understand the Shrine of Los Portales, you must know the history of Seboyeta, also referred to as Cebolleta, which means "little onion" in Spanish. Seboyeta, one of the oldest Hispanic settlements in the area, is located on the east flank of Tsoodzil (Mt. Taylor), the Navajo's Sacred Mountain of the South. Prior to 1720, the Navajo and the Spanish experienced several years of peaceful coexistence. So cordial, in fact, were relations that the Franciscans established a mission in Seboyeta in 1746. The mission was abandoned in 1750, however, when it became apparent that the Navajo weren't interested in religious conversion and tensions mounted.

Location: A tiny town north of Laguna Pueblo.

Description: A hand-carved shrine in the side of a cave, also known as the "Shrine of our Lady of Bernadette of Lourdes" and the "Lourdes of America."

Spiritual Significance: Cave-grotto, spring, Marian Shrine.

Solitude Rating: ★★★★

How to get there: There are no signs to this shrine. Take I-40 to the Laguna Pueblo Exit 114, NM 124. Follow NM 124 to NM 279, across Laguna Indian lands. You eventually leave Laguna lands and enter the Hispanic village of Seboyeta (Cebolleta). The road takes you to Our Lady of Sorrows Church. Wind around the church. The road turns to gravel and quickly goes down a short hill. Turn a sharp left at the base of the small hill. It is a little over a mile from the point where the road turns to gravel to the primitive, dirt parking area for the shrine on your right. Pass through the metal turnstile gate on the left side of the road, opposite the parking area. The dirt path to the shrine is about 75 yards.

Accessibility from highway: Fair, remote.

Facilities: None.

Fee Area: No.

In 1800, as military confrontations increased, additional Spaniards moved into the area and proclaimed their intention to establish a military site at Seboyeta (see Tsoodzil on page 54). Navajo leaders appealed to the Spanish governor not to settle on their sacred mountain, but to no avail. The Spaniards established a military site and constructed a 10-foot wall around the community. The Navajo declared war in 1804 and—in an effort to reclaim their sacred mountain—sent a force of a thousand warriors against the Spaniards.

Many different stories surround the creation of the Shrine. One story claims that village men taking refuge in the cliff overhang carved the altar to express their hope for surviving a siege of "over 5,000" Navajo. Another story tells that the Navajo reduced Seboyeta's Spanish male population to 15 in the earliest days of the settlement. The surviving colonists walked the 1,000 or more miles back to Chihuahua, Mexico, and asked to be sent back to Spain. The viceroy's response was to order them back to Seboyeta to carry out their agreement to colonize the area. They walked back, then erected the shrine to Our Lady of Mercy, vowing to hold feasts each year in her Honor. A third story claims that in the late 1800s, during one of the final Navajo raids, the women and children of Seboyeta took refuge in the cave. The women promised that if their men returned safely, they would build a shrine to the Virgin.

Are all the legends true? None? Pieces of each one? The shrine's namesake, Saint Bernadette, is the Patroness of people ridiculed for their piety, those in poverty, shepherds, and sick people. Bernadette was born a poor, sick girl in France, where she experienced 18 visitations by the Blessed Virgin Mary. On one of these visits, the Blessed Lady told Bernadette to dig in the mud. As she did, a spring began to flow, and she was instructed to bathe in it. From that time, the waters of Lourdes, France, have been considered healing waters. And here you are, far from France, in Seboyeta, New Mexico, at a spring-fed shrine dedicated to Our Lady of Bernadette of Lourdes.

When you walk to this shrine, you feel the powerful presence of the rich and dangerous history. This half-moon-shaped shelter invites the soul-seeker to quiet meditation. Take a seat on one of the four fragile, weathered wooden benches. The carved altar amazes and the religious candles and messages emit hope. A large, nut-brown wooden cross leans into the recessed walls and holy spring-water pools keep company with orange lilies that grow from the barren dirt.

Sit. Breathe deep. Large flocks of swallows fill the sky with dips and glides. This place is an oasis, full of the green growth and fecundity that only water can provide. You know this water has wet the throats of passersby for centuries. This is truly holy water.

In Spanish, *portal* means "porch." Los Portales Shrine probably refers to the way the cave's overhang resembles the porches of Mexican adobe houses. The original statue for this shrine, Our Lady of Sorrows, came from Spain and is now in the mission church at Sebeyota. Was the statue carried from Mexico by the townspeople as they returned from their failed mission to their homeland? Why was it replaced with Saint Bernadette of Lourdes? What healings have taken place here? Mystery abounds at this shrine, with its many manifestations of the Virgin Mary. It is our challenge to quiet the mind, quell the questions, and experience the holy. Leave only prayers.

Other Sanctuaries

Our Lady of Guadalupe Mission, Zuni Pueblo, 505-782-4481
St. Joseph of the Lake Mission Church, Old Laguna Pueblo, 505-552-6654

Retreats

3. Zuni Mountain Lodge

P.O. Box 5114
Thoreau, NM 87323
505-862-7769
zuniml@cia-g.com
www.cig-g.com/~zuniml

A couple days each year, the women in the area's quilting group make their way up the hill to the Zuni Mountain Lodge to finish their annual quilt. These weathered women like the peace and quiet. They relish being waited on, especially by men. And you will, too. I say, without hesitation, that this place is one of a kind. There's no putting on the dog here—no Santa Fe–style saltillo tiles or kiva fireplaces. It's drywall and low-nap carpeted rooms, full of heart and character, with bowls of mini-Tootsie Rolls spread throughout and cuckoo clocks on the walls (although not in the private rooms).

In the late 1970s, Dick Morrow began building this place, and he's still at it. Morrow receives assistance from Bob, the main cook, who whips up hearty breakfasts and dinners, meat-and-potatoes-style, but also accommodates special dietary restrictions. Some of the food is grown in the gardens, and the eggs come from their chickens (when they are laying).

The Zuni Mountain Lodge has seven rooms, some with a view of Blue Lake. Phones and televisions are limited to the communal living room, which is complete with a video library of classic movies and tapes of regional points of interest. Many nooks and crannies offer space to sit and ponder the state of the universe, and the place is a veritable treasure chest of surprises. Behind a chair, you find a bookcase chock full of information on the Southwest, from Native American ceremonials to Turner's book, *Man Corn,* about prehistoric Southwest Indian cannibalism. Jewelry cases are filled with the works of local artisans and the walls are covered with a local painter's work. If you don't find the literal answers to your questions, Morrow is more than ready to offer his engaging point of view.

Tucked into less than an acre of land close to the Zuni Mountains and Wilderness, the lodge is within short walking distance of streams and bird-watching venues. Groups usually bring their own agendas, which the lodge accommodates. A detached meeting room with kitchen facilities is available for classes. Morrow also offers tours of surrounding sites, including ones mentioned in this book: El Morro on page 50, El Malpais on page 48, and Chaco Canyon on the next page.

Location: 31 miles east of Gallup.

Description:
A distinctive inn located above Blue Lake in the Zuni Mountains.

Solitude Rating: ★★

How to get there:
Take Exit 53 from I-40 at Thoreau. Go south on NM 612, 13 miles to the Zuni Mountain Lodge sign on the right at Perch Drive. Turn right and go up the gravel road to the lodge. It's about 0.25 mile up, on your right. Don't expect an obvious sign telling you that you've arrived. It looks more like a large house.

Accessibility from highway: Easy.

Facilities: Convenience store, but no restaurants. The lodge price includes breakfast and dinner. Last gas is in Thoreau.

This place is full of friendly calm. Walk Sister Clare's short Stations of the Cross trail across the forest. Go to the lake to sit and watch the sheepherders bring their woolly friends down to water's edge for a drink. While not recommended for deep retreat, the Zuni Mountain Lodge more than satisfies the need to slow the pace.

Other Retreats

Inn at the Halona, Zuni Pueblo, 800-752-3278
Kokopelli's Cave B&B, Farmington, 505-325-7855
Spirit Ranch Retreat, Lindrith, 505-774-6559

Sacred Places

4. Chaco Canyon, Supernova Pictograph

Chaco Culture National Historical Park
P.O. Box 220
Nageezi, NM 87037
505-786-7014
www.nps.gov/chcu

The Anasazi ruins of the mysterious Chaco Canyon, a World Heritage Site, never cease to amaze and awe. So many unanswered questions surround this place, and there is so much room for the imagination to wander. The Chaco Canyon floor and surrounding mesas are dotted with extensive ruins made of intricate rock work. The largest ruin, Pueblo Bonito, was once the size of the Roman Coliseum, with 600 rooms and 40 kivas. And it's only one of 13 major ruins.

Location: 40 miles northeast of Crownpoint.

Description: A large pictograph of a star, crescent moon, and a human hand, believed to record the supernova of A.D. 1054. You can reach it by an easy day hike, 6.4 miles round-trip.

Spiritual Significance: Some of the greatest surface ruins in the world, petroglyphs, pictographs, great kivas, Fajada Butte, and deep, rich, star-studded darkness.

Solitude Rating: ★★★★

How to get there: From Bloomfield, drive south on US 550/NM 44 to 3 miles south of the Nageezi Trading Post. Turn right onto County Road 7900 at the well-marked turnoff. The road is paved for 5 miles. At the end of the pavement, turn right onto CR 7950 and travel 16 miles to Chaco Culture National Historical Park. This gravel and sand road is bumpy and dusty in good weather, and muddy, slick, and often impassable in rainy weather. Two-wheel-drive vehicles will do all right in good weather. Call ahead for weather conditions: 505-786-7014.

Accessibility from highway: Difficult. The road's a doozy, so hang on to your teeth.

Facilities: Visitor center with bathrooms and drinking water. Camping on first-come, first-served basis. No food, gasoline, or showers.

Fee Area: Yes.

Dominating the landscape and towering 300 feet above the canyon floor is Fajada Butte (*fajada* means "banded" in Spanish), home of the miraculous Solstice Marker. Around 1970, three large, upright rock slabs were discovered near the top of Fajada, placed in front of two spiral petroglyphs. Closer examination revealed that, as the sunlight passed through the slabs during each spring and fall equinox and each winter and summer solstice, dagger-shaped light beams shone upon various points of the spirals. Beams that not only depict knowledge of the yearly solar cycle but, incredibly, the 18.5-year lunar cycle as well. Now research is bearing out that the communities of Chaco Canyon, many miles apart and sometimes out of sight from one another, were also placed on precise lines to mark the equinoxes and solstices based upon the sun's shadow path across the villages. Like the builders of Stonehenge, and the Maya, Toltec, and Inca civilizations, the Chacoans applied the order of the skies to the chaos on the ground and created a complex timepiece of shadow and light to magnify

Supernova Pictograph preserved at Chaco Culture National Historical Park.

cosmic movement. Perhaps as a way to deal with Chaco's unforgiving, grueling summer heat and icy, cold winters.

Chaco features 15 great kivas and more than a hundred small ones. This means that many thousands of people could worship at once. Since no trash heaps and garbage dumps have been found at Chaco, some think that only a few people actually lived in this immense creation of cosmological design and layout. Was it, as many are coming to believe, a site built to magnify and replicate the patterns of the heavens—a place created to exhibit dominance over the landscape, like the great pyramids?

With questions like these, you walk through ancient villages, pass by towering walls ornamented with petroglyphs, and cross sandy streambeds to the cliff wall adorned by the Supernova Pictograph. Take plenty of water on this walk. Wear protective shoes and be sure to wear a hat, especially in the summer, when the sun bears down with severity. (The best thing to do is go early or late in the day!)

The Peñasco Blanco Trail, which leads to the pictograph, begins in the parking lot at the Pueblo del Arroyo ruins on the paved Ruins Loop road. Be sure to get a backcountry pass from the visitor center before you begin. A short way into the walk, you pass the ruins of Casa Chiquita. Then you come upon a side trail on your right that hugs the canyon wall and passes many beautiful petroglyphs. This side trail loops back into the main trail. As you continue to walk, you will see the ruins of Peñasco Blanco on the mesa top, across the valley on the left. The Supernova Pictograph is on the walls below— just follow the signs. You will eventually branch off the Peñasco Blanco Trail and head right onto the pictograph side trail. A short distance away is the sign for the Supernova Pictograph. Look up. Voilà—and *wow!*

And just what *is* this beautiful, deep-red hand, moon, and star you gaze upon? An image of a supernova, the explosion of a large star. At night, if you look into a telescope at the constellation Taurus, you'll see the milky mass of the Crab Nebula. The formation you see is 90 percent of the remains of the supernova—which first appeared around July 4, 1054—that this pictograph supposedly depicts.

The exploding star that created the Crab Nebula was much bigger than our sun. This supernova became visible 6,300 years after the Crab Nebula explosion actually occurred. That's how long its light took to reach our skies—and when it did, a star six times brighter than Venus appeared in the sky, visible day and night for 23 days. The Chinese and Japanese recorded the appearance of this "guest star." To a society such as the Chacoans, whose reality revolved around the cosmos, it is most certain that they recorded it as well. And there's more. A few years after the 1054 supernova, Halley's comet made a blazing, notable appearance. In the pictograph, look below the star, hand, and moon, a little to the left, and you will see three concentric circles, approximately a foot in diameter, with large red flames trailing to the right.

Every 18.5 years (a lunar cycle), the moon and earth return to the same positions they were in on July 4, 1054. When the moon is in the position pointed to by the fingers of the hand, you can situate yourself with a telescope below the pictograph, and then use the drawing to aim your telescope at the large star in the pictograph. When you look into the telescope, you'll see the Crab Nebula.

Once you arrive at the pictograph, you will most likely have this miracle to yourself, as you sit in awe in the midst of the cosmic maze known as Chaco. In the Peñasco Blanco ("white rock point" in Spanish) ruins above you, recent evidence of cannibalism (as in other Chacoan sites) suggests that early descriptions of the Chacoans as a placid, farming society were way off mark. Just who were the people of this place, where few seemed to live but many visited? A people who seemingly put their total existence into creating a cosmic weaving of their lands?

Two-and-a-half centuries—12 generations—after the Chacoan society began, they sealed the doorways and windows, burned the kivas, and departed in a methodical, lengthy exit. You would be hard put to find a place of greater power and mystery than this.

If you want to journey farther into the deep cosmos, the visitor center has a major telescope for night sky viewing. The Chaco staff is committed to the preservation of the night sky and the prevention of light pollution.

5. El Malpais National Monument, Sandstone Bluffs Overlook

P.O. Box 846
Grants, NM 87020
505-783-4774
www.nps.gov/elma/

El Malpais, which means "badlands" in Spanish, consists of more than 17 miles of staggering, jagged lava flows. The Acoma, Laguna, Zuni, and Ramah Navajo peoples continue the land's traditional uses, still gathering wild greens, piñon nuts, and acorns. Here, their valued yucca fruit grows and they collect pollen for ceremonies, pay respects, and renew their ties to these strange, mysterious lands. To the Ramah Navajo, the black chunks of lava represent the clotted, dried blood of Ye'iitsoh, a monster who terrorized the Navajo and killed their people. Legend holds that Changing Woman's twin sons, Born for Water and Monster Slayer, killed Ye'iitsoh with bolts of lightning on Tsoodzil (Mt. Taylor). El Malpais is also, therefore, "where big enemy god's blood clotted."

Location: About 30 miles south of Grants.

Description: Aesthetic, weather-carved sandstone bluffs that meet the dramatic lava beds of El Malpais.

Spiritual Significance: Ancient Indian lands, sandstone formations, lava beds, the place to watch the sun go down.

Solitude Rating: ★★★★

How to get there: Travel east from Grants on I-40 to NM 117. Take NM 117 south several miles to the sign for Sandstone Bluffs Overlook. The parking area is about 1 mile away on a gravel road.

Accessibility from highway: Easy.

Facilities: Bathrooms.

Fee Area: No.

Among the many places to experience El Malpais, you'll find a beautiful natural arch farther down the road and several walking and hiking trails into the lava beds, caves, volcano rims, and lava tubes. I chose the bluffs on the eastern side of the monument for the drama of the stark, black, serrated lava meeting the soft, curving sandstone, creating a provocative tension that launches the imagination. Leave your car, walk to the cliffs, and find a place to sit. This is an exquisite place to meditate and watch the setting sun. Tsoodzil (Mt. Taylor), a Navajo sacred mountain, dominates the northern landscape (see Tsoodzil on page 54).

The ancient peoples of El Malpais lived in outlying communities connected to Chaco Canyon, 80 miles to the north. When Chaco was abandoned in the late 1100s, the communities around El Malpais continued to thrive and evolve into today's Acoma, Laguna, Zuni, and Navajo villages. These badlands have been worshipped and walked for centuries. Sit on the bluffs, gaze west, and hear the ancient whispers.

6. El Morro National Monument

Route 2, Box 43
Ramah, NM 87321
505-783-4226
www.nps.gov/elmo/

*I*n Spanish, *el morro* means "the headland" or "the bluff." El Morro is a dramatic rock, 2 miles in girth, lunging from the landscape. You can see it from a great distance, and the closer you get, the more beautiful it becomes. Definitely visit early in the morning or in the off-season. All the sitting places are on the only trail, so if you want solitude, plan ahead.

The trail length is a little more than 2 miles, at approximately 7,450 feet with a 200-foot elevation gain. Wear shoes with good grip and do not go on top of the mesa if there is a threat of lightning. In the summer, watch for rattlesnakes. The mesa-top trail is closed in the winter months, so call ahead to ensure access.

This is one of the most beautiful, powerful places I have experienced. For thousands of years, people have been drawn here by the permanent water holes on the trails that connect the Zuni and Acoma Indian pueblos with the Rio Grande corridor. Within a short distance of the visitor center, you come upon the silent pool that nourishes all who pass. It's even more amazing when you consider this water is not the result of a spring, but of snowmelt and rains. And it never goes dry. At its most plentiful, the pool is 12 feet deep and contains 200,000 gallons of water.

The signatures of Inscription Rock begin here. As people came to drink—Indians, Spanish explorers, American soldiers, immigrants, even early-day businessmen on their way to California—they carved their record in the stone. I saw no women's words. Is it they who carved the stars? You can borrow a self-guided tour booklet at the visitor center and read about the inscriptions in detail. I recommend that you do the entire hike first, however, without tainting your vision with the pamphlet's words. Walk through this magical place and soak in the images. The handwriting is exquisite, portraying the forthrightness of the souls behind the words. The petroglyphs include bear claws and sheep. The birds and wildflowers are plentiful. As you round the end of the bluff, the valley opens before you, and you walk through ponderosa pine and Gambel oak. A peregrine falcon nest sits on the ledge high above you.

After the short, steep climb to the top, the trail follows the ledge of a narrow box canyon. As you walk the soft rock to the Pueblo Indian ruins, the beauty is almost more than the senses can bear. The ruins, called *A'ts'ina,* "writing on the rock," were occupied during the 13th and 14th centuries by at least a thousand people. In many places, you're standing on the second floor of what were originally three-floor structures. These ruins contain both a round kiva and a square kiva.

I remember having an autograph book as a child, excitedly pursuing the inscriptions of friends and family. This place is an autograph book of the early souls who traveled these lands. Juan de Oñate, New Mexico's first colonizer and governor in 1598, signed the rock in 1605. It is the earliest of the *dated* inscriptions, the first to follow the Indian petroglyphs. In 1906, additional inscriptions were forbidden.

Location: 40 miles southwest of Grants.

Description: A large sandstone bluff with a dependable water hole that has quenched the thirst of people for centuries as they passed through the area and carved their signatures in the soft sandstone. An exquisite hike on top of the mesa, along a dramatic box canyon, takes you to Indian ruins.

Spiritual Significance: Pool, rock mesa, ruins, petroglyphs.

Solitude Rating: ★★★

How to get there: From Grants, take NM 53 approximately 40 miles southwest.

Accessibility from highway: Easy.

Facilities: Visitor center contains water and bathrooms; camping area in the park. It's a long way from a gas station.

Fee Area: Yes.

7. Rock with Wings (Tsé Bit' A'i)

Shiprock Pinnacle
Shiprock

The Rock with Wings was formed 27 million years ago by a volcanic vent. To the Navajo, it is the centerpiece of sacred and mysterious stories. One origination myth tells that once, very long ago, the Navajo were threatened by their enemies. As the healers prayed for the people's safety, the ground began to rise, lifted them away from harm, and placed them in the present location of the Shiprock Pinnacle, where the Navajo settled. They journeyed down from the rock only to plant crops and collect water. Then one day a fierce storm moved in. Lightning struck the rock, destroyed the trail, and formed a sheer cliff that trapped many people high upon the mountain, where their bodies and spirits still remain, not to be disturbed.

Some legends describe the rock as a giant, once-magnificent bird that brought the ancestral Navajo people to these lands. Others speak of the Great Spirit, who sent a stone ship to carry their people to this spot. According to another, the Navajo emerged at this spot, where the stone ship stands as a symbol of their voyage.

As you gaze upon this blood-red sandstone formation, you cannot escape the rock's power as it links earth and sky and brings one closer to spirit.

Location: Around 13 miles southwest of the town of Shiprock.

Description: A stark and inspiring 1,700-foot volcanic rock plume that rises from the desert flatlands.

Spiritual Significance: Sacred place and pilgrimage destination of the Navajo.

Solitude Rating: ★★★★★

How to get there: Rock with Wings is off-limits to everyone but the Navajo, so it must be viewed from a distance. From Highway 666, the pinnacle is six miles to the west. (Or, take NM 64 west from Farmington.) Turn left on Navajo 571, drive down a ways, and stop. This dirt road gives you a good, close-up view of the monolith. Turn around to exit. Note: You are on Navajo lands; do not leave the roadways.

Accessibility from highway: Fair.

Facilities: In the town of Shiprock, a few miles away.

Fee Area: No.

8. Tsoodzil (Mt. Taylor)

Mt. Taylor Ranger District
1800 Lobo Canyon Rd.
Grants, NM 87020
505-287-8833

In March 1864, after 20 years of warfare between the Navajo and the U.S., the Navajo were defeated. They were driven east from their ancestral lands and imprisoned at Fort Sumner and the Bosque Redondo Reservation on the Pecos River. After four years of famine, death, and disease, the Indians were granted return to their lands. On June 18, 1868, they dressed in their best clothing and departed on what is now known as the Long Walk. On July 5, they passed through Albuquerque. On July 6, they crossed the Rio Grande and came within view of their sacred landscape. When they saw their sacred Tsoodzil, it is said that they fell to their knees in tears. Home again.

In Navajo belief, First Man and First Woman built seven sacred mountains. Four of these marked the Navajo universe: Tsisnaajini (Blanca Peak in Colorado) to the east; Doko'oosliid (the San Francisco Peaks in Arizona) to the west; Dibentsaa (Mt. Hesperus in Colorado) to the north; and Tsoodzil (Mt. Taylor) to the south. First Man and First Woman secured Tsoodzil to the earth with a great stone knife, and then adorned her with turquoise, female rain, and plentiful game. They placed a dish of turquoise that held two bluebird eggs on her peak and covered it with buckskin to make them hatch.

The story of Tsoodzil's many names reflects the struggles of the peoples who lived on this land. To the Navajo, *tsoodzil* means "big, tall mountain," and her ceremonial name of *Dzil Dotlizi* means "turquoise mountain." Mt. Cebolleta, or "little onion," was the old Spanish name for this mountain (see Los Portales Shrine, page 39). Anglos named her Mt. Taylor, after President Zachary Taylor, who presided over the U.S. government's war with the Navajo.

There is no mountain quite like this mountain. You see her from afar, as her flanks spread for multitudinous miles into dominating buttresslike mesas. Then, as if by magic, you get close and her peak disappears. While especially sacred to the Navajo, she is holy to many tribes, including the Laguna, Acoma, Hopi, Zuni, Cochiti, and Santo Domingo. She is a place of ceremony and shrines, the source of medicinal plants, and home to hunted game. She is hallowed to many, from head to toe.

Location: Northeast of Grants, this mountain spreads for miles in the San Mateo Mountains.

Description: The Navajo Sacred Mountain of the South, at 11,301 feet.

Spiritual Significance: Mountain, volcano, sacred Native American lands.

Solitude Rating: ★★★★★

How to get there: Tsoodzil is 15 miles northeast of Grants. To get there, exit I-40 at Grants. Take NM 547 from town and follow the signs to Mt. Taylor (it's well marked). At the ranger station office on this road, you can inquire about possible destinations, depending on how far up the mountain you want to go.

Accessibility from highway: Easy to remote.

Facilities: Various campgrounds and bathrooms.

Fee Area: No.

This mountain sees few visitors—if you walk the summit's Gooseberry Spring Trail, you are not likely to see anyone. The moderately strenuous trail is about 6 miles long. Or, with a four-wheel-drive vehicle, you can drive to a high saddle. From the peak, you can see for more than 100 miles. The grassy slopes of the southwest give way to dense forest of spruce, fir, and aspen on the north and east.

This mountain, however, doesn't require reaching the high places. Any place on Tsoodzil will do. Find a place to sit. To be quiet. To feel the force of this mountain. To close your eyes and hear the bluebirds, newly hatched from their bowl of turquoise.

Spiritual Events

9. Shalako Dance

Early December
Zuni Pueblo

The Shalako Kachina dance is part of a 49-day reenactment of the Zuni emergence and migration myths, as well as a prayer for rain, health, and the well-being of the people. It also celebrates the end of the old and start of the new year, and blesses all new houses erected that year on the pueblo. During the dance, spirits of the dead return to be honored and fed.

Shalakos are six giant, masked couriers of the Rain Deities, one for each kiva. Other 10-foot figures include Sayatasha, Rain God of the North; Hututu, Rain God of the South; and Sholawitsi, the Fire (Sun) God. A year before the event, dance participants are chosen at the winter-solstice ceremony. They spend the year learning the long, complicated chants, while the houses that will receive and honor the Shalakos must be built or remodeled.

One elder of the Zuni Pueblo explained, "The whole land is our church; our shrines and religious spots are like the altars in your church." The Zuni believe their ancestors are mediators between mortals and gods. Their Sun and Rain priests secure the rain; the Kachina priests bestow fecundity.

This all-night dance is unsurpassed in color, design, mask artistry, and spectacle. The Shalako Dance is a marvel you will never forget. As you follow the Shalakos from house to house, remember that you are both a guest and a spectator. Be prepared to stand for long periods in extreme cold. And when the clowns or Zuni Pueblo officials ask you to do something, there's no room for discussion (see How to Behave, page 21).

Many visitors stay until 1 or 2 a.m., retreat to Gallup 34 miles to the north, then return for the impressive dawn ceremonies. Because of previous rude outsiders, this event is not always open to the public. Call 505-782-4481.

Other Spiritual Events

Go-Jii-Ya Feast Day, mid-September, Jicarilla Apache Reservation, 505-759-3242

Yei-Be-Chai Healing Ceremony, early October, Navajo Reservation at Shiprock, 505-786-5302

Opposite:
Petroglyphs by
ancient peoples
endure at Chaco
Culture National
Historical Park.

Region Two

North Central:
The Holy Heart

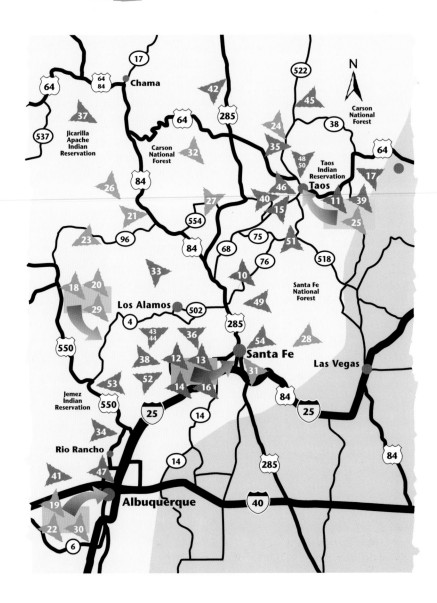

Sanctuaries

10. El Santuario de Chimayo .... page 61
11. Islamic Musalla 64
12. La Capilla de San Ysidro Labrador 66
13. La Conquistadora Chapel and Shrine 68
14. Loretto Chapel Miraculous Staircase 71
15. San Francisco de Asis Church 74
16. Santuario de Nuestra
    Señora de Guadalupe 76
17. Vietnam Veterans National Memorial
    Chapel of Peace and Brotherhood 78
Other Sanctuaries 79

Retreats

18. Bodhi Manda Zen Center 80
19. Center for Action and Contemplation,
    Tepeyac Guest House 82
20. Father Fitzgerald Center 84
21. Ghost Ranch 86
22. Hidden Mountain Zen Center 88
23. La Foresta 90
24. Lama Foundation 93
25. Mabel Dodge Luhan House
    Inn and Retreat 95
26. Monastery of Christ in the Desert 98
27. Ojo Caliente Mineral Springs Resort 100
28. Our Lady of Guadalupe
    Benedictine Abbey 103
29. Riverdancer Retreats 107
30. Spiritual Renewal Center 108
31. Upaya Zen Center 110
32. Vallecitos Mountain Refuge 112
Other Retreats 114

Sacred Places

33. Cerro Pedernal (Flint Peak) 115
34. Corrales Bosque Preserve 118
35. D.H. Lawrence Memorial 120
36. Frijoles Canyon 122
37. Heron Lake 125
38. Kasha-Katuwe Tent Rocks
    National Monument 128
39. Kit Carson Memorial
    Park Cemetery 131
40. La Vista Verde Trail,
    Rio Grande Gorge 133
41. Petroglyph National Monument,
    Rinconada Canyon 135

Sacred Places continued...

42. San Antonio Mountain 138
43. Shrine of the Stone Lions 141
44. Tsankawi Indian Ruins 143
Other Sacred Places 144

Spiritual Events

45. Cambalache 145
46. Las Posadas 146
47. Mass Ascension,
       Hot-Air Balloon Fiesta 147
48. Procession of the Virgin 149
49. Saint Francis of Assisi Feast Day 150
50. San Gerónimo Day 151
51. San Lorenzo Feast Day 153
52. Santo Domingo Feast Day
       and Green Corn Dance 154
53. Zia Pueblo Feast Day 155
54. Zozobra 156

*T*his mountainous region extends in a large V-shape from south of Albuquerque, north to the Colorado border. From the Jemez Mountains to the west and the Sangre de Cristo Mountains to the east. It is the busiest, most heavily populated region covered in this book, encompassing the capitol of New Mexico, Santa Fe, along with Taos and Albuquerque. The Holy Heart region also includes the highest number and greatest variety of retreats, many of the deeply moving pueblos of the Rio Grande, and a seemingly infinite number of narrow streets overflowing with art galleries, and merchants selling handmade crafts and furniture. Many of your travels through this region will be among mountains—sky islands awash in a sea of aridity. Here, you will travel along narrow roads through old Hispanic villages. Here, no matter what route you take, you will encounter hauntingly beautiful sanctuaries and missions, Penitente *moradas,* roadside shrines, and hints of pastoral days and a harsher but simpler life.

Golden eagles grace the sky. Aspen leaves flicker in the wind. And although you must work a little harder to find solitude, when you do, you will be astounded at the wondrous feast this region offers.

Sanctuaries

10. El Santuario de Chimayo

Chimayo, NM 87522
505-351-4889

*E*l Santuario is an awe-inspiring little chapel set in the verdant village of Chimayo, which was settled by the Spanish in 1692. People have been coming to El Santuario, ever since it was built in 1813, to be healed of ailments and infirmities. It is a beautiful place to pray, beseech, give thanks, and meditate. With more than 300,000 visitors each year, chances are slim that you will be alone.

From the very beginning, El Santuario has been steeped in magic and miracle. The lands around Chimayo are an important part of Tewa creation myth. Hot springs, believed to be sacred, were called Tsimajopokwi (*pok-we* is Tewa for "pool of water"). When the healing waters dried up, they were called Tsimayo, which eventually came to be Chimayo.

The Spanish began to settle in the valley around 1700. By 1800, a handful of families lived in the isolated valley, including a family headed by Don Bernardo Abeyto. According to legend, during Holy Week in 1810, Bernardo Abeyto, a Penitente, was performing his usual penance in the nearby hills when he suddenly noticed a strange light, several hills away. He went to the light and saw that it came from the ground. He started to dig and found a wooden cross with the carved image of Our Lord of Esquipulas, the Black Christ of Guatemala. (Esquipulas, a village located in southeastern Guatemala, is where the Black Christ is housed in a white, baroque sanctuary. The sanctuary has been known as a place of miraculous healings since the 1500s.)

Location: In the heart of Chimayo, 30 miles north of Santa Fe.

Description: An adobe church built in 1813, a destination for spiritual pilgrims.

Spiritual Significance: Sanctuary, the "Lourdes of America."

Solitude Rating: ★★

How to get there: From Española, take NM 76 east to Chimayo. The sanctuary is in the middle of the village, just off the highway.

Accessibility from highway: Easy.

Facilities: Food, gas, and lodging in the village of Chimayo.

Fee Area: No.

Twice, Don Bernardo, along with a priest from Santa Cruz (a village to the south) and others, formed a procession and took the cross to Santa Cruz. Each time, the cross mysteriously returned to its original site in the hills. After a third return, they interpreted the occurrences to mean that the cross should remain at its place of origin in Chimayo. Don Bernardo Abeyto built the chapel to house the miracle and dedicated the shrine to Jesus Christ of Our Lord of Esquipulas.

As you enter El Santuario, you enter another world. Five *reredos* (altar screens) and numerous *bultos* (carvings) take you back to a time of beautiful simplicity and show you the way to a world full of promise and answered prayers. Note the two *reredos* as you enter the church, one to the left, one to the right. Another is behind the main altar. The *bulto* of the man on horseback is El Señor Santiago, saint of the warrior and horse, a popular saint of New Mexico. The mysterious crucifix still stands on the chapel altar. Behind the main altar through a door to the left is El Posito, the "sacred sand pit" where Don Bernardo Abeyto first found the crucifix. Here, you can take a handful of the sacred earth, considered to have healing qualities. The Prayer Room, in the sacristy of the church and next to the pit, is adorned with crutches and braces left behind by the healed. In this room you see heartfelt, handwritten notes of thanks and personal testimonies, many directed to Santo Niño de Atocha, the holy child believed to wander the countryside at night, rendering errands of mercy.

Visitors kneel in prayer on the sacred earth, rub themselves with the healing dirt, or even eat it. During Easter Holy Week, hundreds pilgrimage barefoot for miles to El Santuario's doors, to give thanks and to ask for what they need. My friend Mary went to El Santuario and asked to become pregnant—and she did.

11. Islamic Musalla

509 Ranchitos Rd.
P.O. Box 4247
Taos, NM 87571
505-758-1843

*O*ver the course of four years, Michael and Latifa Weinman built this lovely, domed mosque in their backyard so the Islamic community in Taos and traveling Muslims would have a place to pray. *Musalla* means "prayer place," and the doors to the musalla are open to all who wish to come and pray to God, no matter what their religious inclination.

One-fifth of the world's population is Muslim. Of the 10 million or so Muslims in the United States, about a dozen live in Taos. All Muslims, followers of the religion of Islam, are called to prayer five times each day, determined by the position of the sun, beginning with the first light of dawn. On Friday, the major prayer day, the community gathers to hear a short sermon and pray together, followed by a social time of tea and conversation. Unlike most religions in the United States, there is no official head of the church, such as a rabbi, priest, or minister. The community asks a person of knowledge to deliver the sermon. As the saying goes, "Butter floats on milk...everyone knows who these people are."

This is a picturesque and unadorned place of peace and power. You are first met by magnificent handmade doors with a calligraphic inlay that translates, "There is no God except God." Two Muslim boys, 15 and 16 years old, carved and constructed these doors while apprenticing in carpentry north of Questa. The carving and inlay took two years to complete.

Before entering, please note the short list of guidelines posted by the door. Remove your shoes and enter through the doors into a dome-shaped room with an adobe brick floor and mats. A small alcove orients you to the direction of the holy city of Mecca, the direction of prayer for all Muslims. If you happen to enter when others are present, join the others according to your gender: men toward the front, women toward the back.

This little musalla welcomes you to peace and prayer. Copies of the Koran, the Islamic book of guidance revealed through the angel Gabriel to the Prophet Muhammad, are available for you to read. Try Thomas Cleary's translation, which is very accessible and beautiful. It is fascinating to note that every Muslim commits all or parts of this text to memory.

In addition to a place of prayer, the Weinmans also use this place as a classroom for others to come and learn about Islam, a gathering place on feast days of Islam, and as a place of retreat. Within the community, the musalla is also used for funerals, weddings, and a special prayer for rain. Instruction in Islam is available.

Location: In the middle of Taos, just west of the plaza.

Description: A simple and very beautiful place of prayer for those who practice Islam and for all who wish to come and pray to God. The doors are open every day.

Spiritual Significance: Islamic place of prayer.

Solitude Rating: ★★★★

How to get there: From the Taos Plaza, head west on Ranchitos Rd. for less than 0.5 mile. Continue to 503 Ranchitos Rd., on your right. There is a small parking lot in front of the musalla.

Accessibility from highway: Easy.

Facilities: Parking and water (a restroom is planned).

Fee Area: No.

12. La Capilla de San Ysidro Labrador

Cerro Gordo Street
Santa Fe

As often happens, I was on my way somewhere else when I happened upon this striking little chapel, perched on top of a cliff, high above the street. I immediately turned around and looked for a place to park. I had to—this *capilla* (chapel) is one of those places you just can't drive by.

In the early 1920s, when Lorenzo Lopez, Sr., was 60, he began to shape the stones and form the walls of this chapel. A farmer and *santero* (maker of religious images), his creation was dedicated to San Ysidro, the Patron Saint of Farmers and Workers. It took four years for Lopez to finish this testament to his faith. Until Lorenzo's death in 1949, the chapel was the centerpiece of a large, annual, springtime community celebration in honor of San Ysidro.

La Capilla de San Ysidro Labrador sits upon a short, steep rock a little way above the street. Simple stone steps lead to the top, where a plaque announces the site is "Protected by Historic Santa Fe Foundation." Signs invite you to visit and to bring a candle if you wish, but to please respect the space and not leave behind personal items.

And what a space this beautiful, earthy little chapel is. The stone and mud walls are about 18 inches thick, and the entrance is a creative swinging latilla gate. The inside is dominated by a juniper tree growing out of the cliff side into the chapel. I had the feeling this place was built by San Ysidro Labrador himself. A poor, uneducated farmer of the 12th century, San Ysidro dressed like a hermit, and he worked on Sundays, despite the Lord's warning not to do so. After several warnings, followed by grasshoppers and torrential rains, the Lord threatened San Ysidro with "bad neighbors," which finally did the trick. San Ysidro consented to rest on the Sabbath, whereupon the Lord sent an angel to help him plow the fields.

The neighborhood surrounding the chapel is dotted with old windmills that still twirl round and round. La Capilla de San Ysidro is a symbol of the times, not that long ago, when these lands were lovingly farmed. San Ysidro is invoked for affairs relating to agriculture, good weather, and even picnics— all central to the life and well-being of those who work the land.

Location: In the heart of Santa Fe, less than two miles east of the plaza.

Description: A handmade, private chapel of adobe and stone built into the side of a cliff.

Spiritual Significance: Shrine to San Ysidro, Patron Saint of Farmers and Workers.

Solitude Rating: ★★★★★

How to get there: Take Alameda St. east from the plaza. Turn left onto Gonzales St., then turn right onto Cerro Gordo St. The little chapel sits on a cliff above the street, near address number 1154. There is no parking area.

Accessibility from highway: Easy.

Facilities: None at the site, but everything is in Santa Fe.

Fee Area: No.

When Señor Lopez died, the chapel suffered a period of neglect and deterioration that coincided with the decline of farming in the neighborhood. In the 1990s, Ramon José Lopez—highly acclaimed artist, *santero*, and grandson to Lorenzo—spearheaded an effort to renew interest in La Capilla. With the help of family and friends, he formed Cofradía ("Brotherhood") de San Ysidro, raised funds, and restored the chapel. Whenever possible, Lorenzo's original tools were used for the restoration. Today, Lopez family descendants live in the neighborhood surrounding the chapel.

The restoration rekindled the May procession honoring San Ysidro. As you approach the little chapel, you are greeted by a grotto containing a *bulto* of the Virgin Mary with the words, "En Memoria de Todos las Madres" (In Memory of all the Mothers). The *bulto* was created in the spirit of Lorenzo, who Grandson Ramon says intended a special tribute to mothers, but was unable to finish.

(Thank you to the Historic Santa Fe Foundation for the historical information as well as their protection of this very special place.)

13. La Conquistadora Chapel and Shrine

St. Francis of Assisi Cathedral
213 Cathedral Place
P.O. Box 2127
Santa Fe, NM 87504
505-982-5619

Location: In the heart of Santa Fe, just east of the plaza.

Description: A cathedral built by Archbishop Jean Baptiste Lamy, dedicated to St. Francis.

Spiritual Significance: Oldest Marian Shrine in the United States; our country's oldest Madonna.

Solitude Rating: ★★★

How to get there: On Cathedral Place, just east from the southeast corner of the Santa Fe Plaza. Visible from the plaza, the huge, beautiful edifice looms before you.

Accessibility from highway: Easy.

Facilities: Everything is close by in Santa Fe.

Fee Area: No.

$\mathcal{W}$ithin the Cathedral of St. Francis of Assisi is a shrine like no other. You feel her before you see her, the moment you walk through the door from the busy streets of Santa Fe, as you move towards the shiny, impeccably clean and orderly altar, and as you glance at the coat-of-arms banner that reads "Love One Another Constantly." There she is, in the background, tucked away amidst candles in her ancient side chapel. All 31 inches of her beckon you to come closer and hear her tale. She is La Conquistadora, the Blessed Virgin Mary, Our Lady of Unconquered Love. She stands tall above you in the heart of a candlelit shrine that emits solace and exquisite magnificence. And she has a story to tell.

Shortly before Christmas 1625, a Franciscan priest brought her wooden character to the parish church in Santa Fe. At the time, it was common practice for Spanish colonists to bring images of the Virgin to New Mexico. The familiar images comforted the new settlers and helped the friars convert Indians to Christianity. When La Conquistadora arrived from Spain, the people immediately fell in love with her. They dressed her to look like the Spanish Queen and named her Our Lady of the Rosary.

Little did the colonists realize just how much they would need her inspiration. The longtime mistreatment and subjugation of the Indian population soon culminated in the Pueblo Indian uprising of 1680. Many settlers were killed and others fled for their lives. The church was destroyed, but Our Lady was saved and carried into Mexico, near present-day Juarez, to await her return. Every year, the exiled colonists carried her from her parish shrine in Mexico to an encampment northwest of town, where they built a temporary shrine of boughs, prayed, and sang. In 1693, Mexican governor De Vargas began his mission to reclaim Santa Fe "beneath the protection" of La Conquistadora. That year, Our Lady was officially named La Conquistadora when the Spanish settlers peaceably reentered Santa Fe. Today she symbolizes the Blessed Mother and her ability to conquer all hearts with faith and unending love.

This story has several similarities to the story of Seboyeta (see Los Portales Shrine, page 39). The strongest similarity, perhaps, is the promise to honor the Virgin every year with a celebration if victory was granted. De Vargas prayed to the Virgin before his reconquest, making such a promise if she would grant him a bloodless victory. Initially, De Vargas was granted his wish. But when he returned with 70 families the following year, his reception was different, and 81 Indians and 21 Spaniards died in warfare. Fulfilling his promise, De Vargas decreed La Fiesta de Santa Fe in 1712 (see Zozobra, page 156). With Our Lady's return, civic leaders since have emphasized the colonists' original, nonviolent return.

Look carefully upon La Conquistadora, and you immediately grasp that she is no ordinary statue. She has a wardrobe to die for and a public schedule that keeps her in the limelight. The last time I saw her, she was adorned in a sterling silver crown with inlaid turquoise. Her dress—one of more than 200 that grace her closet—was turquoise-colored lace. Her outfit changes continually to match the season and celebration. She wears red and green during Christmas, gold and brown in autumn. Her crown disappears in August for the Indian Market, when she wears a traditional Native American outfit that includes a flowered shawl and scarf. Great care and adoration go into Our Lady's everyday life.

As well they should. Her story and symbolism run deep—a river of faith and enduring devotion to cause. There is a move afoot to change La Conquistadora's name to Our Lady of Peace, undoubtedly riding today's atmosphere of revisionist history. It would be a shame to change her name in an attempt to downplay and deny the less politically correct part of her history. For as much as she represents unconquered love, she also represents that part of *all* of us that seeks to conquer. Life is the struggle to live and satisfy the hunger of both desires. A struggle that, in all her glory, she insists we not forget. There's no doubt in my mind—if this Lady had her way, one of her outfits would be a suit of armor, and only she would go unscathed.

Today, one of the priests in charge of the Cathedral is Native American and another is Hispanic. And La Conquistadora smiles upon everyone with unconquered grace.

14. Loretto Chapel Miraculous Staircase

207 Old Santa Fe Trail
Santa Fe, NM 87501
505-982-0092
www.lorettochapel.com

The Sisters of Loretto were in Kentucky when Bishop Jean Baptiste Lamy asked them to come to Santa Fe to establish a school for girls. In 1853, the sisters opened the Academy of Our Lady of Light (Loretto) in the heart of Santa Fe. Although in a harsh and challenging frontier city beset by smallpox, leaky shelters, and scant supplies, their school for girls flourished. In 1873, 20 years after their arrival, work began on a chapel.

If you have been to Paris and stepped inside the small, exquisite Gothic cathedral of Sainte-Chapelle, then Loretto Chapel will feel familiar. Bishop Lamy, whose homeland was France, was fond of Sainte-Chapelle and sought to reproduce it in Santa Fe. He hired a young French architect to design the church. Stone quarried from many miles away and ornate stained glass purchased in Paris traveled via ship to New Orleans, by paddleboat to St. Louis, and by covered wagons on the Old Santa Fe Trail to the chapel.

In a certain sense, the entire chapel is a miracle, a French gem that elicits a very different feeling than the adobe churches of the area. It is the staircase, however, that demands attention. Before the chapel was finished in 1878, Lamy's nephew murdered the Parisian architect in a jealous rage over his wife's friendship with the expert draftsman. Although workmen were able to follow the architect's plans to complete the chapel, there were no plans or drawings showing how to ascend from the ground floor to the choir loft, 22 feet above. No carpenter or builder could solve the problem in a way that did not destroy the exceptional aura of the church. In such a minute space, an ordinary staircase would not do.

And so the legend is born. The Sisters of Loretto made a novena (a nine-day prayer recitation) to St. Joseph, the Patron Saint of Carpenters. On the ninth and final day, a workman appeared to the Mother Superior. His burro stood patiently, loaded down with carpenter's tools, as he told the Mother Superior that he could solve the problem of access to the choir loft. He asked only for large tubs of water, which she supplied. He went to work, soaking wood, and bending the pliable pieces into the staircase that spirals toward heaven.

Using wood not indigenous to the area, the carpenter completed the stairs in about six months. The miraculous staircase he built marvels even the architects of today with its two 360-degree turns and no nails, screws, or visible supports.

Location: Two blocks from the Santa Fe Plaza.

Description: A staircase built about 1880 for the Loretto Chapel, which includes two 360-degree turns and no visible means of support.

Spiritual Significance: Miracle and mystery.

Solitude Rating: ★

How to get there: Two blocks from the southeast corner of the plaza, at 207 Old Santa Fe Trail.

Accessibility from highway: Easy.

Facilities: In the heart of Santa Fe, there's everything.

Fee Area: Yes.

Who was this mysterious man who did not leave a bill? His task completed, he departed as mysteriously as he appeared, leaving a legacy of a smooth, dark brown staircase that soothes the soul and a story of faith that humbles the soul. Look carefully at the magnificent, curved structure, then close your eyes and try to imagine...how *does* the stairway to heaven stand?

The Loretto Academy closed in 1968, and the property was sold. Today, the Loretto Inn stands where the girls once attended school. The chapel is in the hands of a private family who agreed to keep the chapel intact and share the splendor of it all.

15. San Francisco de Asis Church

St. Francis Plaza
Ranchos de Taos
505-758-2754

*W*hen you walk toward this church, you instinctively know you are somewhere special. Be silent and you will hear her breathe. Be still and you can almost see her move as the sunlight falls upon her curves and changes her appearance, moment to fleeting moment. She is vintage Taos—imperfect construction and naïve forthrightness. Her hand-carved, Gothic Revival–style door is very small, out of scale with the huge structure, and the towers are almost amateurish. Her body, in fact, is very much like our own: from the earth, imperfect, and unique. Her form is the common, traditional Latin Cross main body, 35 feet wide by 125 feet long. The adobe walls are 6 feet thick at the base, contouring to 4 feet as they rise to the top. Her great adobe buttresses exude soft strength and magnificent power.

As you stand from afar and view this grand mission, you cannot escape the fact that she looks like a fortress. She was originally built without windows, as protection for townspeople against raiding bands of Apaches, Comanches, and Utes in search of livestock, food, and slaves. Once the danger of attacks ended in the 18th century, the two small windows were added to the church.

The inner sanctum of this edifice is starkly simple. Note the brightly colored *bulto* of St. Francis, Patron Saint of Ecology, the saint for whom this church is named. At the front of the church are two *retablos*, large wooden frames that enclose strikingly beautiful

Location: On the south end of Taos in Ranchos de Taos.

Description: An adobe mission church built between 1772 and 1816.

Spiritual Significance: An incredible edifice considered to be one of the most painted, sketched, and photographed structures in the United States.

Solitude Rating: ★★ (Depends on the crowds—you may get lucky!)

How to get there: In Ranchos de Taos, south of Taos proper, on Pueblo del Sur, the highway to Santa Fe.

Accessibility from highway: Easy.

Facilities: Everything is in town.

Fee Area: No.

paintings of saints and religious symbols. The one on the front altar of the church, most likely painted as early as the late 1600s, came from Spain via Mexico and up the Camino Real in the 1700s. The other, off to the right of the altar, was painted by New Mexico artist Santero Molleno in the early 1800s. Take a seat in the simple, wooden pews. Let your eyes feast upon the thick, earthen walls and tree-lined ceilings (*vigas*). You feel as if you are a piece of a special secret.

Parishioners are buried in the flower-filled courtyard, where benches invite you to sit and commune with the statue of St. Francis. Or, visit in the winter, when snow lines the majestic curves, assuming an angle of repose.

Be sure to walk across the plaza to the church rectory to see *The Shadow of the Cross,* a painting by Henry Ault. By daylight, it depicts Christ standing on the shore of Lake Galilee. In darkness, the portrait becomes luminescent and the clouds over the left shoulder of Jesus form the shadow of a cross. Ault painted this several years before the discovery of radium, the radioactive element that glows in the dark. Therefore, many people call this 1896 work a miracle. What do you think?

16. Santuario de Nuestra Señora de Guadalupe

100 Guadalupe St.
Santa Fe, NM 87501
505-988-2027

$\mathcal{I}$mages of Our Lady of Guadalupe are seen virtually everywhere across New Mexico—on the sides of buildings, in private yards, painted on the trunks of cars, and embellishing white cotton T-shirts. I carry her star-studded image, standing upon a crescent moon, on my key chain. She is the dark, virgin Aztec Goddess of Mexico, La Virgen Morena, Patroness of the Poor and Disenfranchised. She is also a potent symbol of justice and Hispanic identity.

This church, built between 1776 and 1796, sits at the end of the Camino Real, the Royal Road that served as the principal trade route between Mexico City and her northernmost outpost in New Mexico. The grueling, 1,700-mile journey took six months each way. On one of these arduous journeys in 1873, Jose de Alzibar's altar painting traveled in pieces from Mexico City via a mission-caravan mule train. The trains, which usually numbered three per year, consisted of 32 *carros* (large, heavy freight wagons) pulled by eight mules each. Today, the *reredos* is a stunning backdrop for the many services and concerts that take place in this beautiful chapel.

The Santuario de Nuestra Señora de Guadalupe is a haven in the heart of Santa Fe. Although today it is a secular building, its small, quiet meditation chapel to the right of the altar area is heavily used by residents and travelers alike as a place to be still and silent. Mass is still celebrated on December 12, the feast day of Our Virgin of Guadalupe, and also held at 12:12 p.m. on the 12th day of every month. Art exhibits, live performances, and concerts take place in El Santuario, including the world-renowned Santa Fe Desert Chorale. If you're lucky enough to be in Santa Fe at Christmas, the chorale's holiday concert of high artistry fills the chapel with sacred song amidst the 4-foot-thick adobe wall acoustics.

This church has withstood fire, neglect, and even plans to raze her and build a parking lot. Praise be that wiser intent prevailed.

Location: In the heart of Santa Fe.

Description: A shrine to Our Lady of Guadalupe.

Spiritual Significance: The oldest existing shrine to Our Lady of Guadalupe in the United States.

Solitude Rating: ★★★

How to get there: In the heart of Santa Fe at 100 Guadalupe St.

Accessibility from highway: Easy.

Facilities: Everything is in Santa Fe.

Fee Area: No.

17. Vietnam Veterans National Memorial Chapel of Peace and Brotherhood

Angel Fire, NM 87710
505-377-6900
www.vietnamveteransnationalmemorial.com

This memorial stands at 8,500 feet like a great white angel spreading her wings across the Moreno Valley. As you drive up the hill and approach the memorial, however, a full-size Huey helicopter first catches your eye. At first glance, it appears to be crashing, but it is actually taking off in its familiar pattern of clearing the ground and angling as soon as possible to avoid fire. To Vietnam veterans, this helicopter is synonymous with the war itself, given its critical role in protection, transport, and supply.

As you pass the helicopter and walk down the sidewalk along the mountainside, you see a small memorial plaque on the right, dedicated to Victor David Westphall III, who was killed in ambush in 1968. David's family took dirt from New Mexico and placed it where David died in Vietnam. Likewise, they brought dirt from Vietnam and mixed it with native soils.

The Chapel of Peace and Brotherhood is a cavernous, terraced place of tranquility with seating rows built down into the mountainside. Small cushions and boxes of tissues dot the curved, unadorned inlaid-stone *bancos* (benches), from which you look upon a simple cross. A narrow, floor-to-ceiling window offers a peak at the outside world. Once you enter, step down, and take a seat, you become oblivious to the curious folks who also enter and pass through. Here, you can sit as long as you desire.

If you wish to journey further into the history of the Vietnam War, the 6,000-square-foot visitor center contains a veterans' room filled with items donated by Vietnam veterans and their families, a photo gallery of the men and women killed in Vietnam, an ambush display, a library, a large photographic exhibit of scenes from Vietnam, a tribute to the women who served in Vietnam, and computers to assist veterans with information on the whereabouts of loved ones.

The Vietnam Memorial is a nonprofit project, dependent upon private donations. On the off-season, weekday morning that I was here, there was a constant stream of visitors. Clearly, what began as a family's tribute to their lost son hit the nerve of a nation, which continues to grapple with this war of incomprehensible pain. This chapel and memorial are testimony to the great contradictions of war, as the Westphall family honors the lost, acknowledges the anguish, and points the angels toward peace.

Location: About 25 miles east of Taos.

Description: This beautiful, nondenominational chapel was built in memory of Victor David Westphall III, who was killed in ambush in Vietnam in 1968. The chapel is open 24 hours a day, year-round.

Spiritual Significance: An "enduring symbol of the tragedy and futility of war."

Solitude Rating: ★★

How to get there: Take US 64, 4 miles north of Angel Fire.

Accessibility from highway: Easy.

Facilities: Chapel, visitor center, bathrooms.

Fee Area: No.

> Greed plowed cities desolate
> Lusts ran snorting thru the streets
> Pride reared up to desecrate
> Shrines, and there were no retreats.
> So man learned to shed the tears
> with which he measures out his years.

—From "The Ultimate Curse" by David Westphall III
(written before he departed for Vietnam)

Other Sanctuaries

Congregation Albert, Albuquerque, 505-883-1818

Pardes Yisroel Orthodox Synagogue, Santa Fe, 505-989-7711

San Felipe de Neri Church (1792), Albuquerque Old Town, 505-243-4628

San Miguel Mission, Santa Fe, 505-983-3974

St. Augustine Catholic Church, Isleta Pueblo, 505-869-3398

Retreats

18. Bodhi Manda Zen Center

P.O. Box 8
Jemez Springs, NM 87025
505-829-3854
www.bmzc.org

*T*hree spiritual/healing retreat centers in this book are located on the Jemez River within a short distance of one another. One of the most fascinating things about these very different centers is the way they unfold their aspirations upon the riverside landscape, between deep canyon walls, and in the shadow of the Virgin Mesa, which looms above them. The Bodhi Manda Zen Center does this very beautifully. If you come in the summer, you will see tall fields of corn and small, Buddha-adorned spring-fed pools with large orange carp moving through the depths and water lilies sprouting on the surface. The locals raise much of their own food here, keep their own chickens for fresh eggs, and grow flowers that dance and delight. I doubt you've ever seen a Cosmos flower garden like this one, complete with zippy hummingbirds.

Against this background is a quiet, contemplative center of serious practice begun in the mid-1970s by Zen Master Kyozan Joshu Roshi of the Rinzai lineage. Thirty-seven years ago, Joshu Roshi came to this country from Japan to "spread the true seed of Buddhism." Now in his 90s, he continues to travel to this center from California twice a year to lead spring and autumn retreats.

Daily practice at the Bodhi Center consists of waking up early to sit, chant, and meditate. Working, eating, sleeping, and being is in "full relationship" with all. The center's purpose is to create a place to come and experience the harmonious environs of flora and fauna, while exploring the nature of birth and the world in which we live. Instruction and guidance are available in this structured retreat center, where practice takes place year-round.

Summers at Bodhi Manda are filled with retreat groups that come from across the country, from different religious denominations and backgrounds. Dormitory lodging is available for groups. Fall, winter, and spring are more conducive to individual retreatants who are invited to come, take instruction, share in hearty vegetarian meals, and soften the boundaries between self and universe. The last two weeks of June, the center holds a seminar on Buddhism consisting of classes and study. Each month is highlighted by a full-moon sitting meditation. And neighbors claim the three-day New Year's celebration and the New Year's Eve sit are absolutely wonderful.

Guests, retreatants, and students, are all welcome at the center. There is a guest house with four private rooms and baths, and guests are free to share in the meditation schedule, meals, and work around the grounds. Please call ahead.

No matter your spiritual orientation, you will find a special greeting at Bodhi Manda… small and intimate in acres and numbers, but very large in heart.

Location: In the heart of Jemez Springs.

Description: A Rinzai Zen practice center on the Jemez River. Structured retreat in the heart of the Jemez Mountains at 6,000 feet.

Solitude Rating: ★★★★

How to get there: NM 4 is the only highway into the canyon, from the north or south. In the village of Jemez Springs, look for signs to the Zen center on the west side of the road. The office is located a few yards off the highway.

Accessibility from highway: Easy.

Facilities: In Jemez Springs.

19. Center for Action and Contemplation, Tepeyac Guest House

P.O. Box 12464
Albuquerque, NM 87195
505-242-1846
www.cacradicalgrace.org

*F*ather Richard Rohr, a Franciscan priest, founded the Center for Action and Contemplation (CAC) in 1987. Rohr was committed to creating a contemplative center where spiritual endeavors could meld with social justice issues. Since then, thousands of people have taken part in CAC retreats and programs. In June 1990,

Location: In the city of Albuquerque.

Description: An old adobe retreat home, in a semirural residential neighborhood, committed to rest and rejuvenation in an atmosphere of simplicity and nonviolence. A center for both structured and unstructured retreat at 5,000 feet.

Solitude Rating: ★★★

How to get there: From I-25, take the Cesar Chavez exit and go west. This turns into Bridge Blvd. Go right (north) on Five Points Rd. to Tepeyac, which is on the right. The center is at 1705 Five Points Rd.

Accessibility from highway: Easy.

Facilities: Everything is in the city.

the center expanded its outreach to include a separate retreat house. The retreat, called Tepeyac, is named for the hill deep within Mexico where Our Lady of Guadalupe first showed herself to Juan Diego. This house was formerly the "motherhouse" of the Franciscan Province of Our Lady of Guadalupe.

Tepeyac guest house is available for individual and small-group retreats, both structured and unstructured. The house can accommodate up to 12 people in a communal living setting. Bedrooms are private and cozy, while the remainder of the house and gardens is shared. A hearty breakfast is included in the low, nightly cost. The kitchen is available for additional meals and all meals are vegetarian.

The CAC chapel and office is located up the road about 1 mile from Tepeyac. In addition to intern programs in engaged spirituality, they offer workshops in areas such as contemplation and ecology, contemplative enneagram, and rites of passage for men and women (separate retreats). You can stay at Tepeyac as part of one of their programs or come as a solitary retreatant and never leave the grounds.

The focus at Tepeyac is on simplicity, quiet, and sustainability. Body work such as yoga and massage are available upon request. The 1-acre grounds feature a small worship room, a grand old cottonwood tree, and "the girls," a group of chickens that cluck and scratch and provide the center's eggs.

If you are looking for a place that encourages directed spirituality, a caring place that is steeped in social justice issues, then CAC and this retreat house have much to offer. Subscriptions to "Radical Grace," the center's bimonthly newspaper, are available for $14 per year.

20. Father Fitzgerald Center

P.O. Box 10
Jemez Springs, NM 87025
505-829-3586
www.theservants.org

*T*he Jemez River Valley is called the Dark Canyon. Perhaps the title is literal, perhaps metaphorical, for undoubtedly many "dark" events occurred within the confines of the dazzling stone cliffs, where the ancient Jemez people lived in many villages spread along the river bottom and mesa tops. One such village was Giusewa, which contained the San José de los Jemez Church. During the Pueblo Rebellion of 1680, the Jemez people attacked the church to destroy the Catholic presence, killing the priest and setting the church on fire.

Across the street and within view of this historical site, the large, modern chapel of the Fitzgerald Center stretches towards the light of the sky as if to reach beyond the shadow. More than 50 years ago, Father Gerald Fitzgerald created the Fitzgerald Center as a center of rest, healing, and renewal for troubled clergy of the Catholic Church. It is interesting that Father Fitzgerald, somewhat of renegade himself, chose this site of historic tension and struggle—qualities that permeated the Center through its rocky years of transition from a treatment center to a retreat center for all faiths. Today, the Fitzgerald center opens its doors to all individuals and groups seeking a place to be in solitude and to restore the spirit.

The center has accommodations for up to 36 people, including suites and a single hermitage. As a day-use conference center, its various meeting rooms can accommodate up to 45 people. The center serves meals family-style in a group dining area. The grounds also include tennis and basketball courts, a hot tub and pool, and river access.

A daily worship service is available for those who wish to participate. The exquisite shrine and church, built in 1962 in honor of Mary, Mother of Priests, is available for quiet and meditation. For those who wish to climb the Virgin Mesa, the Center provides exclusive access to a beautiful trail to the mesa top, sacred homeland of the ancient Jemez Indians. Even this trail is not without a story of fallen dreams; it is dedicated to Sister Joan Deleplane, who prepared for priesthood in the 1970s, at a time when it seemed as if Vatican II would make such dreams a reality. Upon beginning her studies, her students and staff presented her with a plaque that read, "I will go where there is no path and I will leave a trail." Alas, it was never to be, as beloved Pope John XXIII died and another stepped into the Shoes of the Fisherman. This trail is the perfect place to reflect on dreams, paths and hopes—in the spirit of Sister Joan.

Location: On the north end of Jemez Springs.

Description: An unstructured Catholic retreat center, at 6,000 feet, run by the Servants of the Paraclete for the purpose of reflection, relaxation, and renewal.

Solitude Rating: ★★★

How to get there: On NM 4, across from the Jemez State Monument, just north of the village and hot springs of Jemez.

Accessibility from highway: Easy.

Facilities: In Jemez Springs.

21. Ghost Ranch

HC 77, Box 11
Abiquiu, NM 87510
505-685-4333
www.ghostranch.org

*W*hen you enter Ghost Ranch in the heart of summer, the first thing you notice is the verdant fields and rust-red mesas. The second thing you notice is the busy-ness and bustle of the place. You'll feel as if you've entered the middle of an anthill—where every being has a purpose—and you, too, will soon have yours! This is midsummer at Ghost Ranch, its busiest 10 weeks, filled with families, fascinating programs, and class participants from across the country. Fall, winter, and spring, however, are slower and more easygoing—much more conducive to solitude. Off-season visitors drop from summer's 400 maximum to an off-season maximum of 125.

When you come to Ghost Ranch, you come to a place of special history and beauty. Old-timers call it the Ranchos de los Brujos, or Ranch of the Witches, believing it to be haunted by evil spirits. Ghost Ranch is located on 21,000 acres, not far from Georgia O'Keeffe's home in Abiquiu. O'Keeffe fell in love with the ranch landscape and spent many summers here. She eventually purchased a house and 7 acres within the ranch for a summer place; here, she walked and painted the high-desert lands.

Ghost Ranch, one of the few family-centered retreat centers, offers accommodations and facilities for 400 men, women, and children. The schedule is packed with fascinating course offerings for the spiritual seeker, including An Advent Retreat, Circle of Women, Healing Earth, Healing Ourselves, Icons and Santos, Praying with the Mystics, Sacred Individuality, and Spirit of Place. The ranch also offers a vast assortment of courses in the arts, photography, and natural history. A swimming pool and many hiking trails lie within this breathtaking terrain. Vegetarian and traditional meals are served in a central dining hall. Accommodations consist of camping areas and modest, comfortable rooms with shared baths. For the individual retreatant who seeks a solitary experience, I suggest making reservations after Labor Day—perhaps even after November, when the flurry of summer activity dies down and winter sets in.

Location: About 16 miles northwest of Abiquiu.

Description: A Presbyterian conference and family retreat center tucked away among splendiferous high-desert mesas at 6,500 feet. Structured and unstructured retreat, including day visitation or overnight accommodations.

Solitude Rating: ★★★

How to get there: Look for signs on US 84, northwest of Abiquiu, between mileposts 224 and 225.

Accessibility from highway: Easy.

Facilities: Inclusive retreat facility. No gasoline.

Whether you visit Ghost Ranch for a day or a week, do not pass up the opportunity to walk the incredible labyrinth located on the east end of the compound across from the new arts center. This structure, designed after the famous Chartres Labyrinth, is a 0.5-mile circular path for the purpose of prayer, meditation, and reflection. Like the kabala of the mystical Jewish tradition and the Hopi medicine wheel, labyrinths connect us to that deeper part of ourselves as we walk the path to the metaphorical center of the soul. Approach the labyrinth in silence and reverence. You may focus on a specific question as you walk. Or, leave the experience open and unguided to see what revelations fall into the space of your contemplative journey.

Ghost Ranch, and the Monastery of Christ in the Desert a few miles away, give the spiritual retreatant a rich choice of facilities. One with myriad activities and classes to further the spiritual journey, the other with nothing but empty, silent space. One where you may bring your family and find enriching activities for everyone, the other where you come alone and hear only your own breath. Both set within breathtakingly beautiful landscapes.

22. Hidden Mountain Zen Center

216 Ninth St., NW
Albuquerque, NM 87102
505-248-0649
www.peacemakercommunity.org/hiddenmountain/

A special challenge faces those creating a haven of peace and solitude in the middle of the city. Cities require that you stay somewhat guarded and contracted, while wilder, natural settings encourage openness and relaxation. In the busy, traffic-filled city, you don't have the solitude of nature to help still the soul. And yet, without a doubt, a city is where a haven is most needed. Amidst these special challenges, Hidden Mountain Zen Center makes its statement, providing an extensive program of Zen practice on two adjoining properties within beautiful, old restored homes.

Zen Buddhism originated in China 1,200 years ago. In its simplest form, the religion teaches the art of deep introspection into our true natures, toward lives of peace, simplicity, and compassion. From the moment you take off your shoes and enter the door at Hidden Mountain Zen Center, a thick and beautiful calm envelopes you. This is a small, intimate setting. You will rarely practice with more than 10 people. In summer, they hold intensive three-month retreats, in which you can participate wholly or partially. Daily *zazen* (sitting meditation) is open to the public, as well as various offerings such as Living Through Cancer Workshop; Women, Menopause and Zazen; and lessons in Chinese calligraphy. Zazen instruction is available during most scheduled zazen sessions, but please call in advance. The center's members are also involved in a youth mentorship program for children who have an incarcerated parent. On-site lodging is available, and the vegetarian meals are prepared and eaten in a communal setting.

The Zen Center's resident teacher is Jitsudo Sensei, a native of northern New Mexico, who returned to his homeland from California in 1999 to become head abbot of the center. Hidden Mountain welcomes all to come and learn the Zen Buddhism tradition—to experience deep peace within the bustle of the city.

Location: In the city center of Albuquerque.

Description: This structured retreat center for the practice of Zen Buddhism sits smack in the middle of the city in a quiet residential neighborhood just beyond the downtown business district.

Solitude Rating: ★★★

How to get there: From I-25 in downtown Albuquerque, go west on Martin Luther King Blvd. Take Martin Luther King Blvd. to Ninth St., and then turn left (south). Continue to 216 Ninth St.

Accessibility from highway: Easy.

Facilities: Everything is in the city.

23. La Foresta

P.O. Box 145
La Jara, NM 87027
505-289-3025
www.laforesta.org

Location: Northeast of Cuba.

Description: Structured and unstructured retreat, in the high-mountain forest at 8,000 feet, with emphasis on sanctuary for caregivers, especially those who work with the dying: families, social workers, hospice and AIDS workers, etc. You may work for your stay in lieu of monetary payment.

Solitude Rating: ★★★★★

How to get there: Take US 550/NM 44 to Cuba; 4 miles north of Cuba, turn north onto NM 96 and drive 2 miles into La Jara. Turn right on County Road 496 (FR 28), across from the post office, and follow the paved road for 5 miles to a T. Turn right at the T, and drive a short distance to the gate for La Foresta and the La Foresta at La Jara Creek Ranch sign.

Accessibility from highway: Easy.

Facilities: Last gas and food is in Cuba.

St. Francis (ca. 1181-1226), the Patron Saint of Ecology, is traditionally depicted in a long robe with birds on his shoulder and a wolf at his feet. He was one of those souls who puzzled the church bureaucracy, a renegade who chose a different path from the traditional, hierarchical settings of worship. The Church wasn't quite sure what to do with him. He chose to be and live with the people in a simple life with no possessions, much as the Gospels recommend. In so doing, St. Francis of Assisi became one of the most important saints of the church—a symbol of simplicity, love, and the philosophical life. In his later years, sick and exhausted from overwork, St. Francis would not leave his people to care for himself. It took an order from the bishop to force him to rest. Bound by his vow of obedience, he retreated to a hermitage, Santa Maria de la Foresta, deep in the Italian countryside. And so it is with those who serve others: It often takes an order from on high or a collapse from exhaustion to force them to stop, rest, and direct their caregiving towards themselves—to go to La Foresta.

New Mexico's La Foresta is a simple, beautiful place. In true Franciscan spirit (the order named for the followers of St. Francis), it is the perfect place to rest the weary. Deep within mountain wilderness at an altitude of 8,000 feet, the crystalline air fills the lungs and clears the mind. Birdsong heals the soul and quiet softens the hard, worn shoulders accustomed to carrying the weight of the world. The forest is tall, the ebony night sky full of stars. From the moment you enter the gate and see Isabo and Hildegard, the two resident donkeys, you know you are in a special place.

La Foresta's 70 acres are nestled within millions of acres of public forests. The grounds include a pond, large open meadows, hiking trails, and old-growth forest. One hiking trail takes you through aspen and giant oak to a high-meadow meditation bench where you can see Tsoodzil (Mt. Taylor) in the distance, sacred mountain of the Navajo (see Tsoodzil, page 54). The large ranch house features bedrooms, a beautiful kitchen and communal eating area, a glass meeting- and prayer-house, hot tub, sauna, library, and art studio with musical instruments. La Foresta houses 20 people comfortably, but you can come as a hermit, if you wish, remaining separate and preparing your own meals.

Warmth and heart is the way of the staff. Your blue-jeaned host, Father Michael, a follower of St. Francis and a member of his order, seems too young to know the firsthand costs of grievous stress. His work in New Orleans with AIDS patients brought him to this deeply personal commitment to provide a haven for those who do the hard work with the dying—to create a place like no other retreat.

Without a doubt, Michael has succeeded. While groups and individuals can come to take part in the many structured Caregiver Weekends, La Foresta is also open to anyone who needs rest and respite from the workaday world. Everyone, on some level, is a caregiver, and all are welcome here to come and do nothing but nurture the soul. Rest, read, walk, sleep, paint, write, and daydream. No personal agendas or religious themes overlay the landscape. If you desire pastoral counseling or assistance with spiritual direction, it is available. If you want to take part in chanting, drumming, prayer, meditation, or sacred walks, or if you want help with stress manage- ment, it is here.

But there is no expectation that you will do anything other than come and let the earth's healing cycles be your guide. Sleep in the moonlight and hear nature's silence. This simple, comfortable retreat holds you dearly against the mountainside.

24. Lama Foundation

San Cristobal, NM 87564
505-586-1269
lama@compuserve.com
www.lamafoundation.org

A narrow, winding, gravel road marked with tattered prayer flags shows the way up Lama Mountain to your destination. If you have problems with high altitude, then Lama may be difficult. Located at 8,600 feet, Lama features commanding views of the San Luis Valley, the Rio Grande Gorge, and, in the far distance, San Antonio Mountain. The location alone encourages an open heart and contemplation.

Lama, located on 105 acres, is bordered on the north, south, and east by national forest. In May 1996, a wildfire destroyed 95 percent of Lama's vegetation. Charred, ebony tree spines protrude from the mountainside, a constant reminder of death and regeneration. And regeneration there is, as human hands join nature's push to create anew.

The feeling at Lama is one of voluntary simplicity with a strong dose of 1960s hippie. With few modern conveniences, they tout themselves as a rustic, land-based community. They admit, however, that the challenge is great because of a growing season of only 90 days and strong, prevalent southwest winds.

Lama's program is splendid, whether you're looking for a structured, spiritual group opportunity or the solitude of a hermit's retreat. Classes include varied options such as straw-bale construction internships for

Location: North of Taos in the Sangre de Cristo Mountains.

Description: A community devoted to a diversity of spiritual practices toward their vision of awakening consciousness; structured and unstructured retreat at 8,600 feet.

Solitude Rating: ★★★★

How to get there: Take NM 522 north of Taos. Turn west after mile marker 15, immediately after the lumberyard (or from the north, 4 miles south of Questa). Cross the cattle guard, then follow the signs up the mountain.

Accessibility from highway: Fair to difficult.

Facilities: Simple shelters and outhouses, but no gasoline or electricity.

women, yoga intensives, Gurdjieff movement and dance, and gay and lesbian spirituality gatherings.

Two hermitage cabins are available for solo retreat. Once you arrive and settle in, hermits (that's you!) do not interact with anyone else. The cabins are stocked with whole, bulk foods, such as nuts, nut butters, teas, coffees, and cereals. You can bring your own food, but there is no refrigeration. Every other day, someone checks to see if you need food, water, or juice, and replenishes your food stocks. Other accommodations at Lama include a tipi and a cabin, with plans to build another. For a decreased fee, you can visit Lama as a volunteer and assist in the many projects. Tent sites are available for those who wish to visit but not volunteer.

Resounding bells announce the communal meals held in the main dining room and on a spacious porch overlooking the Rio Grande Valley. The food is luscious, simple, vegetarian fare, introduced with a ritual song and a hand-holding circle of thanks.

Lama's visitor list is impressive. In the early 1980s, Father Thomas Keating's retreat here evolved into the Chrysalis Movement, a Catholic network of service communities devoted to prayer and contemplative life. Ram Dass finished his book, *Be Here Now*, in collaboration with the Lama community. "Sufi Sam," Samuel Lewis, looks down on Lama's central area from high above, where he is buried.

A special feeling exudes from a place free of the electromagnetic chatter of power lines, where a curtain of dark embraces at nightfall. This is the experience of Lama—a place to access your soul, free of technological interference.

25. Mabel Dodge Luhan House Inn and Retreat

240 Morada Lane
Taos, NM 87571
800-846-2235
www.mabeldodgeluhan.com

Location: In Taos, a short walk from the central plaza.

Description: An intimate retreat inn—packed full of characters and the ghosts of characters. Structured and unstructured retreat in the center of Taos at 7,000 feet.

Solitude Rating: ★★

How to get there: From the Taos Plaza light in the center of town, go east on Kit Carson Road (US 64) to Morada Lane, two blocks down. (Look for signs at the turnoff—it's very close to the plaza.) Continue on the narrow, winding Morada Lane for a short distance to the parking area on your left. Look for the wooden stairs that take you up the small hill to the inn.

Accessibility from highway: Easy.

Facilities: Everything, since you're in the middle of town. No phones or televisions in rooms.

*M*abel Ganson Evans Dodge Sterne Luhan is one of the many Taos eccentrics who lives long beyond her death. She came to Taos in 1918 and purchased this property a few short months after her arrival. Before Mabel hit Taos, however, she had lived a flamboyant, exciting life that only the rich could create. From her villa in Italy, she entertained the likes of Picasso and Gertrude Stein. Then she moved to New York and held court over a salon in her home in Greenwich Village, where the world's renowned thinkers, radicals, and artists filled her home with lively conversation. She continued to feel, however, that her life was "all form, no content." So she sent her fourth husband, Maurice Sterne, to Santa Fe in order to paint and explore Indian life. Sterne lured Mabel to the Southwest, and she immediately fell in love with the landscape and native people, sure that she had found the place where her soul would find peace.

From the moment you step onto this 5-acre estate, you feel a certain calm. Perhaps it's the adobe rooms, full of spirits past. Perhaps it's the

shape of Mabel's old home, designated as a National Historic Landmark, which invites you to travel from room to room through short, beautiful arches. Mabel's house is a place where people come, rest, and become deeply involved in their "work," whether it's a class they come to participate in or individual, unstructured time away from the norm.

It's hard to believe this inn and retreat is in the heart of Taos. Los Gallos, as Mabel called the house in honor of the ceramic roosters that still grace the roof, is surrounded on two sides by Pueblo land. It was the land that her final husband, Pueblo Indian Tony Luhan, said she must have. The 18 bedrooms here possess the personalities of the famous folks who once frequented them, including Willa Cather, Georgia O'Keeffe, Ansel Adams, and Mary Austin. Choose Mabel's room and sitting area on the second floor, and you sleep in the grande dame's hand-carved, spiraled bed. Sit by her kiva fireplace and take in a view of the mesa that spreads and connects to the nearby Sangre de Cristo Mountains. Mabel and Tony believed, in fact, that Los Gallos was a direct power spot for the energy of Taos Mountain, which is sacred to the Taos Pueblo Indians.

Mabel was served breakfast in her bedroom while the other guests— and there were always guests—ate where you eat today, in a picturesque communal kitchen and dining area. A hearty breakfast is included in the stay of every private guest; groups can arrange as many as three meals a day. You can take part in a variety of writing, photography, art, and meditation workshops, or you can arrange to bring your own group to Los Gallos and have it all to yourself. If you come here alone, there are nooks and crannies, indoors and out, where you can sit and relax. Next door, at Illumina Gallery, you can roam and wander the exquisite sculpture garden with its tiny waterfalls and meditation lake.

There is something special about staying at a place where Carl Jung and Martha Graham stayed. D.H. Lawrence painted those crazy designs on the glass windows upstairs. See the white cross standing far out back in the field? Georgia O'Keeffe painted that cross. Rumor has it that Tony set his tipi up outside the house at the base of Mabel's staircase. But before there were staircases, there were ladders, inside and out.

Try to stay in a room in the big-house area. The separate guest house offers the lowest prices, but the rooms do not have the ambience of the main house, and it is a short walk away (perhaps an advantage for some). I was especially charmed by the Robinson Jeffers Room, and, of course, Mabel's.

26. Monastery of Christ in the Desert

Abiquiu, NM 87510
guests@christdesert.org (for reservations)
www.christdesert.org (for more information)

The hermit life has long been the epitome of holiness. Saint Benedict, for whom this monastic order is named, was born near Spoleto, Italy in A.D. 480. From his solitary life, often lived on mountains and in caves, he came to believe that work and prayer should be indistinguishable. Benedict also believed the physicality of work, prayer, and reading should hold equal places in one's life.

Three Benedictine monks, traveling west from the Mount Saviour Monastery near Elmira, N.Y., founded this monastery in June 1964. The first monks came to stay 10 years later, in search of the Benedictine life that revolves around St. Benedict's spiritual centerpiece of prayer, reading, and manual labor. Today, the 30 or so monks live as a family that chooses to see God together. Apart from the world, but still part of the world. Their life is a contemplative one, based upon their vows of obedience, conversion of life (which includes vows of chastity and poverty), and stability of place.

When you walk upon these grounds, you feel and breathe the splendor of these vows. It's in the stillness. In the curving simplicity of the buildings. In the wooden and stone sculptures that caress the landscape. In the gentle voices of the men who welcome you. You know, instinctively, that you are in an extraordinary place. A place at the end of the road, an apt metaphor for the wearied, searching, or hungry soul.

People of every spiritual orientation are invited to Christ in the Desert. You may come here as a drop-in day visitor or make reservations to stay for longer periods. If you're planning a visit, leave electronic gadgets and musical instruments at home, but do bring a flashlight, wind-up alarm clock, and clothes for weather extremes. No shorts are allowed in the chapel, refectory,

Location: About 75 miles northwest of Santa Fe or 53 miles south of Chama.

Description: Contemplative, unstructured, silent retreats with a family of Benedictine Monks in the remote setting of the resplendent Chama River Valley at 6,000 feet above sea level.

Solitude Rating: ★★★★★

How to get there: Turn west (left) onto FR 151 from US 84, 17 miles north of Abiquiu. Take the narrow, gravel road for 13 miles until you reach the entrance. This road is muddy and slick when wet (the rainy season is July and August). Park on the left and walk in to register.

Accessibility from highway: Fair to difficult.

Facilities: Meager, with no phones or gas. Although food is not available for day guests, there are accommodations and hearty vegetarian meals by reservation for 13 guests. Wonderful campgrounds outside the monastery in the national forest on the Chama River, off road 151.

or guest house area. The luscious, vegetarian meals available to overnight visitors are taken in silence, in the refectory with the monks, who read scripture aloud at lunch and play classical music with dinner.

If you wish, you may participate in the Roman Catholic services. Days pass against the weaving of the monks' liturgical schedule. They meet seven times a day to sing the English and Latin texts. How long has it been since you've heard live Gregorian Chant? The monks encourage guests to participate in work for at least some days of their visits. You can choose tasks that fit your abilities and interests, such as overseeing the gift shop, cleaning, or gardening. The gift shop is a treasure house of handmade items, many made by the monks. The modus operandi of this monastery is silence and low, soft conversation—in addition, each room provides a medallion on a cord that you can wear to indicate that you wish total silence. Walks and hikes in the bordering national forest are plentiful.

The monks believe they change the world through their creation of a community of love. Like the wilderness that surrounds their beautiful realm, it is important to know this haven exists. A place to replenish. A place to seek counsel, if need be. A place just to be, in silence and prayer, at the end of the road. The dead end, where new lives surge, and all travelers wear the face of God.

27. Ojo Caliente Mineral Springs Resort

Ojo Caliente, NM 87549
800-222-9162
www.OjoCalienteSpa.com

I've been visiting the Ojo Caliente hot springs for decades. I go there when I want to immerse my body in waters that heal. When I want to slow down, amidst the soft conversations of others, in a place full of olden spirits. A place free of pretense. This is the only springs in the world where five different types of mineral water erupt from the earth. Those in the know, know it heals body and soul.

Ojo has always been a different kind of place. It's not the place to go if you want to be pampered by attentive staff or beautiful lodging. The rooms and cottages, quaint and adequate, have no phones or extra amenities such as complimentary robes, shampoos, or hair dryers. The newer room I stayed in had no bathtub, shower, or towels bigger than a facecloth. Breakfast is not included in the cost of the room.

When you visit the springs, bring two quarters for a locker if you want to store your valuables, and be prepared to pay a $3 deposit (or leave your room key) for a large, clean towel. I mention this because it may be hard to round up money once you've left your room or car and entered the dressing rooms. When you check in, be sure to ask for the welcome packet, which includes a description of Ojo's waters and maps of the grounds and hiking trails. Ask questions here—don't assume you'll be told everything you need to know.

Although the "service" part of Ojo may be a bit rough, just remember, you are here for the waters and the expansive New Mexico skies and land-scape. The grounds, covered in beautifully sculpted flower gardens, and the curved concrete paths immediately start to take the edge off stress-encrusted shoulders. A labyrinth outside the main lodge sets the tone for your visit.

And then there are the waters. To protect the atmosphere of spiritual retreat, families with children are segregated into a large, partially covered pool. The remaining pools are for adults only. On weekend mornings, they hold a meditation/chanting hour followed by an aquatic movement hour of yoga and tai chi (free for overnight guests and $5 each for others). These activities take place in the soda mineral spring pool, the only indoor pool. Designated as a "quiet area," the water in this pool is tingly and buoyant.

Admission to the pools (included in the price of lodging) gives you access to all seven pools, an arsenic bath, and a hot wrap. The adult-only arsenic mineral pool spring at Ojo—the only known one of its kind in North America—is believed to help arthritis, rheumatism, burns, eczema, and even stomach ulcers (if taken internally). The water rises from the ground at 113 degrees and is cooled by a combination of open air and cooler spring water. Following your soak in the hot arsenic bath, you're led to a dimly lit room lined with rows of beds. Here, you lay on your back, wrapped mummylike in a cotton blanket topped with a heavier wool cover. The sweat cleanses toxins from your body and every muscle turns to jello. It's a good time to daydream or nap.

Technically speaking, these hot springs rise in a volcanic fault area, where Precambrian granite and quartzite lift and define the west side of the Rio Grande Rift. The temperature ranges from 98 to 113 degrees in these soaking pools—which contain iron, arsenic, soda, and lithium—providing comfort and, many claim, healing. The iron mineral spring, the original pool used for centuries, sits in the open air at the base of a sandstone cliff. The pool has a sandy bottom, reaches 109 degrees, and is beneficial for the blood. The sodium spring, for drinking, is said to be good for stomach problems and arthritis. The lithia spring pump, which emits water at 104

Location: 26 miles north of Española.

Description: An unstructured retreat at a hot springs visited by Indians since the pre-Columbian times.

Solitude Rating: ★★

How to get there: North of Santa Fe on US 285, 1 mile west of milepost 353.

Accessibility from highway: Easy.

Facilities: Gas, food (including meals and snacks in the on-site restaurant), lodging and tent spaces for day visits or extended stay.

degrees, is believed to be good for stomach problems, tired kidneys, and depression. To further nourish your body, Ojo offers a cornucopia of massage therapies, natural skin-care treatments, bio-wraps, and body treatments, all for extra charges. But you don't have to have a fat billfold to come here. While the Ultimate Ojo Luxury Package Treatment lasts four-and-a-half hours and costs $315, you can come in for a quick soak for $9.50, or buy a regular day pass for $18 or a deluxe day pass for $25. (These rates are for Monday through Friday; it's slightly more on weekends.)

In times past, people believed springs were places where spirits from the underworld communicated with those of us on the physical plane. The Ojo Caliente springs exude spirit and history. Tewa Indians visited and used these springs—which they believed to be a gift from God—for hundreds of years. Their ruins still grace the nearby cliffs, where they lived in the 1300s and 1400s. The Spaniards discovered the springs in the 1500s and believed them to be the fabled Fountain of Youth. Explorer Cabeza de Vaca named the springs Ojo Caliente, the "hot eye." In the late 1800s and early 1900s, Ojo was known around the world as a sanitarium. People came to heal their ailments, staying from two weeks to three months, bathing in and drinking the waters.

The Tewa Indians call this place *posee po pee,* "green springs," probably alluding to the algae covering the rocks, turning them emerald green. The grandmother of Poseyemo, a Tewa hero, is said to still live in one spring. Today, a private pool is set aside for tribal elders and other members of the Eight Northern Pueblos.

This is a special place, where history, landscape, and healing waters blend and replenish the spirit. Come here to rest and restore. Journals are available in the gift shop so you can record those unexpected thoughts and dreams that rise to the surface.

28. Our Lady of Guadalupe Benedictine Abbey

P.O. Box 1080
Pecos, NM 87552
505-757-6415
www.pecosabbey.org

Location: 25 miles east of Santa Fe.

Description: A Benedictine monastery, home to both the Monks of Our Lady of Guadalupe Abbey and to the Sisters of the Mother of Mercy and Peace Monastery. Structured and unstructured retreat on the Pecos River at 7,000 feet in the Sangre de Cristo Mountains.

Solitude Rating: ★★★★

How to get there: From I-25, exit onto NM 50 east of Santa Fe or onto NM 63 from Las Vegas, N.M., and go north. The monastery is located on NM 63, a short ways north of Pecos.

Accessibility from highway: Easy.

Facilities: All inclusive. Gas in Pecos.

Like the Benedictine Monastery of Christ in the Desert, when you enter the gates of Our Lady of Guadalupe Benedictine Abbey, a.k.a. the Pecos Abbey, you enter a community of those who devote their lives to prayer. Within this context, you are invited to come, visit, and participate in the prayer life of the monks and sisters. The Benedictines prefer nothing above the work of God, believing the path to God is through prayer. "Everything," says Father Michael, "flows from this God-dimension." For you, the retreatant, participation in the five daily prayer services is voluntary. Your visit can be as simple as being in this beautiful place among people with full hearts. To come here is to let the silence of the river valley and mountains lift the worries from your shoulders.

The Pecos Abbey provides directed and nondirected retreats. The many structured retreats include subjects on yoga and Christian meditation, dreams, loss, the contemplative heart, creativity, spiritual growth, and prophecy. Well known as one of the most intellectually active

Benedictine abbeys in the country, Pecos Abbey features a host of impressive lecturers and spiritual "superstars" such as Ester de Waal and Dr. James Finley.

If you bring your own group and your own program to the abbey, you can use the facility's 30 rooms and enjoy three delicious meals a day. Or, you can come with no agenda. Spiritual guidance and counseling are available, but please mention the need when you make reservations. For the solitary pursuit, the monastery provides four self-contained, very fine and lovely hermitages up and away on a hill, removed from the main collection of buildings. You can rent them by the night—with no minimum or maximum stay—and join others for prayer and meals as you wish. Without a doubt, this abbey offers one of the finest hermitage opportunities in the state.

The 1,100-acre abbey stands gently on the banks of the Pecos River. Ponds and grassy meadows, with many benches and sitting areas, are at your disposal. Cross the footbridge over the river and climb to the mesa above or follow the river along various hiking paths; trails take you north to Monastery Lake. The monastery is surrounded by national forest, featuring birds and ducks galore, including a spirit-lifting kingfisher who fills the riverside with his raspy call.

This place is truly special. Perhaps it is the melding of the 12 monks and 11 sisters and the way they sing across the sanctuary to one another. Perhaps it is the beautiful artwork that adorns the walls. Perhaps it is the smiles and open hearts that greet you, as they have greeted people from all over the world of most every religious and nonreligious background.

29. Riverdancer Retreats

16445 NM Highway 4
Jemez Springs, NM 87025
800-809-3262
www.riverdancer.com

Riverdancer Retreats is a small, peaceful center with a focus on a holistic healing. The great-room lodge with fireplace and the lovely courtyard living quarters are set back, away from the highway, offering beautiful strolls to the Jemez River. This is a place where you can come and do nothing. Or, you can personalize one of several healing packages of alternative health options, such as acupuncture, breath work, movement, meditation, and massage. People commonly come here to de-stress or to help their recovery from chronic fatigue syndrome or depression. Riverdancer also offers creative process retreats, workshops, and celebrations, utilizing art therapy, yoga, dance, ritual, and drumming. There is a fire pit and sweat lodge on the grounds down by the river. Meals are hearty, organic, and vegetarian with some dairy. With diet as a major focus of the holistic approach, you won't find sugar or red meat. And of course, the hot springs in Jemez Springs, a mile up the road, assist in the healing process. Myriad trails and beauty exist amidst the prehistoric volcanoes.

Location: On the south end of the village of Jemez Springs, 60 miles north of Albuquerque.

Description: Structured or unstructured retreat opportunities in a beautiful center at the base of Virgin Mesa. Offerings include: healing retreat packages to renew and rejuvenate body and soul, retreats for people in treatment and recovery from disease and stress, and facilities for those seeking a quiet, restorative setting for creative endeavors.

Solitude Rating: ★★★

How to get there: Just south of the village of Jemez Springs on NM 4, look for the sign on the west side of the road.

Accessibility from highway: Easy.

Facilities: In Jemez Springs.

The feeling here is one of quiet elegance and pampering. It is a wonderful place to visit and stroll among the giant cottonwood and ponderosa pine. To sit by the river and write, sketch, or daydream. And if you need an extra lift to the spirit, just sit and watch the hundreds of hummingbirds zip around the courtyard.

30. Spiritual Renewal Center

2348 Pajarito Road
Albuquerque, NM 87105
505-877-4211
www.christdesert.org/dominican/

Location: Temporarily housed in a pastoral setting, on the south end of Albuquerque.

Description: A personal and group retreat center of the Dominican Sisters who follow their order's motto: "To contemplate and to give to others the fruits of contemplation." Structured and unstructured retreat, at 5,000 feet.

Solitude Rating: ★★★

How to get there: Take I-25 south to Rio Bravo Blvd. Take this road west to Isleta Blvd., and turn south (left). Continue about 3 miles to the well-marked Pajarito Rd., and turn right. The center is 0.5 mile on the left.

Accessibility from highway: Easy.

Facilities: In the city.

The 90-year-old hacienda that houses the Spiritual Renewal Center will be a lonely place when the perky Dominican Sisters leave for their new location on Coors Road. Until then, they are putting the chapel, dining room, and grounds to good use. They claim their food is home-cooked and delicious, and by the satisfied faces of the partakers, I believe them. It is clear that this center is run by devotion, hard work, and grit—and the results are something to brag about!

The Sisters offer structured and unstructured retreat. For the private retreatant seeking solitude and a space for prayer, they set aside a private bedroom and provide dinner. With 31 beds available at the center, hermits are welcome. The day begins at 8:30 a.m. with prayer, though it could just as likely begin with yoga or tai chi.

The center's varied programs include offerings such as silent prayer and fasting, enneagram weekend retreats, dream retreats, food-addiction 12-step weekends, and extended retreats for women or men. The holistic retreat includes a sweat lodge.

The center is closed in August. Be sure to call ahead for reservations and to confirm the location.

31. Upaya Zen Center

1404 Cerro Gordo St.
Santa Fe, NM 87501
505-986-8518
www.upaya.org

The short drive to Upaya is the perfect introduction to this beautiful place of retreat. Narrow roads snake among old adobe buildings and homesteads. Iron windmills from another age turn with the breeze. It's hard to believe you're only a few minutes from the heart of the city—and it's even harder to believe it when you arrive at the small campus of Upaya, tucked into the Sangre de Cristo foothills. From the road, you look down upon their valley lands, adorned with adobe buildings, gardens, and fruit trees.

Upaya is Sanskrit for "skillful means" or the "craft of compassion." Within these definitions, the center offers courses and retreats on engaged spirituality, contemplative care of the dying, Zen training, meditation retreats, and various international retreats. You can take an individual retreat at Upaya, attend their many extraordinary class offerings, or retain the facilities for your personal group use. The grounds can accommodate up to 50 people (with lodging for 30). Daily practice is open to the public, Monday through Friday, from 7 to 8:30 a.m. and 5:30 to 6:30 p.m. Practice includes zazen, chanting, and walking meditation, and on Wednesday evenings, a dharma talk.

Formal retreats are many and varied, including retreats and councils for women with breast cancer, Vipassana and yoga retreats, peace work retreats, and a meditation retreat on the Four Noble Truths, which focuses on stillness and "not knowing."

Location: In Santa Fe, 2 miles east of the plaza.

Description: A Buddhist study center that offers courses and retreats (structured and unstructured) for groups and individuals.

Solitude Rating: ★★★★

How to get there: From the center of Santa Fe, take Alameda St. east. Turn left onto Gonzales St., then right onto Cerro Gordo St. The pavement turns to gravel; in a short distance, you come to address number 1404. Look for the address as there is no sign.

Accessibility from highway: Easy.

Facilities: In the city; all inclusive.

Upaya is especially well-known for its women's retreat, In the Shelter of Each Other, an annual four-day gathering of women that includes storytelling, dancing, music, and meditation with a backdrop of contemplation and social action. This offering, like the majority of the programs, is led by anthropologist Joan Halifax Roshi, the founder of Upaya Zen Center. (Laurance S. Rockefeller and Richard Baker Roshi gifted the Upaya House to Joan in 1992.) The fact that Upaya is well-endowed remains evident in its five beautiful Southwestern, Santa Fe–style, and Asian-style buildings. Artistic, picturesque architecture lies beautifully on the grounds amidst paths that wind and calm the soul. The first Tibetan Stupa in the United States is here. The communal dining area is full of sunlight, and the vegetarian fare is scrumptious.

Upaya Zen Center feels and looks like a little piece of heaven, where the hard and blessed work of spirit continues day to day. Many creative and potent programs emanate from these grounds. A stay here is sure to calm the most harried soul (at about $70 per night for a private room). A sauna and paths through nearby piñon-studded foothills are here too, to ease you along.

32. Vallecitos Mountain Refuge

P.O. Box 3160
Taos, NM 87571
505-751-9613
www.vallecitos.org

Retreats provide a special solution to those who experience burnout, whether from spiritual disconnection, the stress of everyday work life, or undefinable pressure that builds from within. Vallecitos recognizes that those who work in areas of public interest are particularly subject to stress. With long hours and low pay, burnout and tension build, leaving little left over to give to one another, rendering even the strongest good intentions ineffective. Vallecitos is dedicated to creating an environment where those submerged in wrenching issues such as economic justice, AIDS, civil rights, and environmental preservation can come to replenish, rest, and reflect.

This 135-acre mountain refuge is far away from distractions. Power lines do not even exist here, which also means no phones or televisions. As those of us who have lived away from electromagnetic "chatter" know, a special peace comes with the absence of electric wires. An impressive, historic log lodge, solar cabins, yurts, and walled cabin tents blanket the hillsides, accommodating up to 30 people. Vegetarian meals are served communally. The outdoor showers, the classiest rustic showers you're ever likely to come upon, are complete with beautiful forest views. And, in Buddhist tradition, every day includes a period for work.

Location: About an hour's drive west from Taos.

Description: A picturesque ranch deep within Carson National Forest, at 8,500 feet. This structured retreat for contemplation and renewal is specifically designed for those who work in public-interest and nonprofit organizations.

Solitude Rating: ★★★★★

How to get there: West of Tres Piedras and south of Hopewell Lake, several miles off US 64. Contact the Vallecitos office for specific directions.

Accessibility from highway: Difficult.

Facilities: None, once you leave Tres Piedras.

The calm of this place is enough alone to work a special magic. But Vallecitos takes it one giant step further, framing their location with three primary offerings: contemplative retreats, meditation retreats, and a refuge fellowship program. Contemplative retreats invite the participants of nonprofit organizations, innovative communities, and coalitions to come together for contemplation, reflection, and discussion. Their days consist of meditation, silence, meditative hikes, and talking circles that serve as a basis for problem solving and group discussion. These discussions are not about how to solve a specific problem—and are not networking—but give attention to the deeper questions that are rarely addressed, such as inspirational sources and spiritual values. Meditation retreats take silence to its deepest level, with retreatants spending 10 days in silence and meditation with renowned instructors. Silence is not broken until the final day. Retreatants may also apply to the Refuge Fellowship Program, which pays all expenses for a two-week visit to the ranch for established activists and public-interest leaders from around the world. Fifty percent of the fellowships are awarded to people of color. With no agenda for these visits, they provide the opportunity for people who rarely leave their villages or the city to let the mountains work their magic—through talking circles, horseback rides, jumps into rivers and streams, and an occasional chase by the resident beaver who lays diligent claim to his pond. The purpose is to create a time for reflection and an opportunity for rejuvenation and healing for those who share a common vision to make the world a better place. Once a person has participated in a Vallecitos program, they may come and stay at the hermitage for a week in unstructured retreat; meals are delivered and solace assured.

Without a doubt, this place is very special. The 135 acres are surrounded by 300,000 acres of forest land, and the retreat's most mighty teacher may well be one of the oldest ponderosa pines in the region, estimated at between 500 and 600 years old. (The oldest known, in Arizona, is 742 years old.) Eight ponds and many springs await you here, and the Vallecitos River cuts a lush swath below the lodge. This refuge rests upon the mountainside in an air of mindfulness and attention to its natural setting. Their vision of serving those who work to save and protect the planet and their commitment to a contemplative refuge for the people on the front lines is nothing short of valiant.

Other Retreats

Casa Escondida, Chimayo, 800-643-7201

Corkins Lodge Resort & Wilderness Retreat, Chama, 800-548-7688

Heart Seed B&B, Retreat Center, & Spa, Santa Fe, 505-471-7029

San Gerónimo Lodge, Taos, 800-894-4119

Taos Art Retreat, Ranchos de Taos, 505-751-3220

Sacred Places

33. Cerro Pedernal (Flint Peak)

Santa Fe National Forest, Coyote District
Youngsville, NM 87064
505-638-5526

From the first time I arrived in Taos, I kept looking westward asking, "What *is* that peak out there?" She tugged at me from more than a hundred miles away. She captured my imagination and wouldn't let go. I *had* to travel across the vast desert and mountain landscape to find her. And the closer I got, the more cryptic and powerful she became, changing form from a high, flat-topped volcanic cone to a straight-up, pointed spike to a slanted, chimneylike top. This is Cerro Pedernal, the shape-shifter of

Location: Southwest of Abiquiu and southeast of Youngsville.

Description: A famous, sacred mountain landmark of the Southwest, this peak stands at 9,862 feet. The Tewas call this mountain *tsee peeng ya,* which means "flaking stone mountain."

Spiritual Significance: Volcano; spring; source of flint to prehistoric peoples, Chacoan descendants, and Tewa Indians. Holy mountain, central to the mythology of many Native American peoples. Mesa-top ruins called *Tsi-p'in-owinge',* which means "village of the flaking stone mountain."

Solitude Rating: ★★★★★

How to get there: Take FR 100 south from NM 96 at Youngsville. Travel 5.5 miles to FR 160, marked by a small sign a ways in from the main road. Up to this point, you're on a good gravel road. But from here, proceed only if you have a high-clearance four-wheel-drive. The remaining distance from this point is approximately 3.5 miles. Proceed on FR 160 for 1 mile, then turn left on a spur road. Go 1.1 miles and take a very sharp turn to the right off 160. Look for the word "Cerro" on the large tree on your right. From here, the road is steep and you will definitely need the high clearance—if you don't have it, park. Continue 1.4 miles to the open area on the west side of the base of Cerro Pedernal. This is a great place to camp or backpack and just be with the mountain. If you plan an ascent, it's a good place to stop and rest and prepare.

Accessibility from highway: Extremely difficult and remote.

Facilities: Gas, food, lodging, and restaurants in Abiquiu, a few miles to the east. Developed and undeveloped camping available in the forest around the mountain.

Fee Area: No.

the high-desert terrain, trickster-source of buried treasure stories, and home to hard, strong flint that slices the fingers of those who chip and carve.

The strenuous trail to the top of Cerro Pedernal—which requires rock-scrambling and rope-climbing—is steep, brushy, and sometimes hard to see. Attempt this hike only if you are mountain wise—in good shape, experienced at finding trails, and acquainted with mountain climbing. The trail begins at the major cairn (rock-pile marker) at the end of the road. Look sharp-right for additional cairns that lead you up the mountain on a faint trail. Follow cairns to the base of the upper cliff, and make your own cairns as you continue up the mountain. This is a good place to stop and "be" with the mountain, if you do not wish to complete the final ascent. To continue, traverse around the cliff going south until you reach a nylon rope. A short rope-climb up the cliff connects you with the trail, which continues to the top. *Note:* In the summer, only attempt this hike in the morning. You do not want to be on top when the afternoon thunderstorms move in. There are many lightning-scarred trees up there!

You may know the Pedernal as the peak Georgia O'Keeffe painted over and over again. "This is my private mountain," she was fond of saying. "God told me if I painted it enough, I could have it!" When she died, her friend Juan carried her ashes to the top where, the story goes, he cast them to the wind.

Cerro Pedernal has been the spiritual and physical sentinel of the region for centuries. Her flanks were home to artifacts dated from 7000 B.C., and her white chert has been found east of the Rio Grande in a Paleo-Indian case which is believed to have been used 9,000 years before the birth of Christ. Pedernal is central to the Tewa ancestral lands, to a Jicarilla Apache emergence story, and perhaps even to the story of the birthplace of Changing Woman, one of four primary figures in the Navajo Origin Myth. Pedernal's chert has been found in ruins of New Mexico and Colorado. The mountain has stood high and grand for centuries, while populations came and went below her and one group pushed out another, in the rocky rhythm of this region.

Climbing Cerro Pedernal is a rigorous, dangerous spiritual pilgrimage. Her top rewards you with sweat, exhaustion, and an awe-inspiring, 360-degree view of high desert cliffs and distant mountains. You feel the power of this place amidst the lightning-struck trees. You hear the songs of ancient visitors. As tired as you might be, a strange and wonderful energy courses up through your legs and you want nothing but to walk upon her from end to end. To sit with her. To stay and pray.

34. Corrales Bosque Preserve

P.O. Box 707
Corrales, NM 87048
505-897-0502
http://www.village.corrales.nm.us

*I*f you're looking for a respite from the city frazzle of Albuquerque, the Corrales Bosque Preserve is a glorious place to walk, meditate, and breathe in the calm of nature. If you're staying at an Albuquerque retreat center, it's particularly perfect as a day trip.

Location: On the Rio Grande River, about 20 miles north of Albuquerque, across from the Sandía Pueblo.

Description: A forest and wildlife haven along the Rio Grande River, adjacent to the old, agrarian village of Corrales.

Spiritual Significance: River, cottonwood forest.

Solitude Rating: ★★★★★

How to get there: Take the Corrales Highway (NM 448), the major thoroughfare through the village, to Romero Road, which runs along a large irrigation ditch. Turn east, towards the river, onto a dirt/gravel road and travel to the end (about 1 mile), where there is a parking area. The preserve is open from 5 a.m. to 10 p.m.

Accessibility from highway: Fair.

Facilities: Everything, since you're close to the city.

Fee Area: No.

In Spanish, *bosque* means "forest," and in this case, it's a grand cottonwood corridor, the best example of a vanishing kind of forest, featuring 100-year-old trees that canopy the river's edge. A walk on the wooded trails can afford glimpses of pheasants and roadrunners, plus Canada geese that grace the island. More than 200 species of birds have been identified here, and in the spring and fall, you may well see migrating flocks of cranes and hear their eerie, beautiful, prehistoric call.

Your ever-constant bosque companion is the mighty Rio Grande—the source of life in this arid desert country and the subject of centuries of veneration by the ancient peoples who lived along her shores. Not that long ago, the Rio's shores curved and changed direction for hundreds of miles in regular floods, seeding and creating new life on a constantly changing shore. Today, the river has been straightened and almost drained dry by modern demands. Mighty no more, she is close to losing her soul. Modern man's control having been a success, she has not flooded since the 1940s.

Breathe deep this special place, as it is rare. Offer this river a prayer. Entreat the return of new *bosques*.

35. D.H. Lawrence Memorial

San Cristobal

> Only the big pine in front of the house, standing still
> and unconcerned, alive.... One goes out of the door,
> and the tree-trunk is there, like a guardian angel. The
> tree-trunk, the long work table, and the fence!

> —D.H. Lawrence, *Mornings in Mexico*

*T*his home of D.H. Lawrence during the 1920s never ceases to still my spirit and send my imagination into flight. I've been here several times and always had the place to myself. But the homestead is small, so if people arrive at the same time as you, you will most likely see them. Lawrence originally named his homestead Lobo, meaning "wolf," but later changed the name to Kiowa, after a Taos Pueblo Indian trail.

Here at Kiowa, you feel the days of a writer's life. Lawrence spent most of his time in isolation, writing in the morning, chopping wood, milking his lanky cow, Susan, and baking bread in his self-made oven. Mabel Dodge Luhan lured Lawrence to New Mexico, giving this ranch to his wife, Frieda (knowing Lawrence would never accept such a gift). In return—and to keep their obligations clean—Frieda gave Mabel the original manuscript of Lawrence's *Sons and Lovers.* Although the couple's original vision of a utopian community never materialized, Lawrence settled into a pattern of creative

Location: About 20 miles north of Taos in the Sangre de Cristo Mountains.

Description: Beautiful mountain home of the great writer, D.H. Lawrence, and his wife, Frieda. Lawrence's ashes are contained within his shrine, which overlooks his home at 7,000 feet.

Spiritual Significance: Home of the "inspired ones," where D.H. Lawrence wrote, and prominent painters painted.

Solitude Rating: ★★★

How to get there: The clearly marked turnoff is on US 522, about 10 miles north of Taos. Continue up the gravel road for 5 miles.

Accessibility from highway: Fair.

Facilities: None.

Fee Area: No.

days, completing great works such as *The Plumed Serpent*, and his magnificent novellas, *St. Mawr* and *The Woman Who Rode Away.* Lawrence's poor health shortened his stay in New Mexico and forced his return to Europe in 1925. There, he died of tuberculosis in 1930, at age 44.

Lawrence and his wife Frieda are both buried on Lobo Mountain, a short, zigzag walk up the hill from the homestead. Frieda's third husband, Angelino Ravagli, whom she married after Lawrence's death, designed this shrine. Lawrence's ashes are literally in the walls, the result of an argument between Frieda and Mabel over where to place them. In exasperation, Frieda threw the ashes into the concrete mix, stilling the conflict once and for all!

The author of *Lady Chatterley's Lover* considered his Taos days the best of his life. New Mexico was, for Lawrence, the epitome of a spiritual place:

> I think New Mexico was the greatest experience from the outside world that I have ever had. It certainly changed me forever. Curious as it may sound, it was New Mexico that liberated me from the present era of civilization, the great era of material and mechanical development. Months spent in holy Kandy, in Ceylon, the holy of holies of southern Buddhism, had not touched the great psyche of materialism and idealism which dominated me.... But the moment I saw the brilliant, proud morning shine high up over the deserts of Santa Fe, something stood still in my soul, and I started to attend.
>
> —*Phoenix: The Posthumous Papers of D.H. Lawrence*

The Lawrence Memorial is a place to come and feel where the mind's eye takes flight. Join in commemoration with thousands of others by signing the guest book located in the shrine. Then, find a green, grassy spot, perhaps under the "Lawrence tree" that Georgia O'Keeffe made famous in her painting. Then, sit and listen to spirits past.

36. Frijoles Canyon

Bandelier National Monument
HCR I, Box 1, Suite 15
Los Alamos, NM 87544
505-672-0343 or 505-672-3861

Location: 48 miles northwest of Santa Fe.

Description: One of the most scenic and spectacular canyons in New Mexico.

Spiritual Significance: Cliff dwellings with cave kiva, pictographs, petroglyphs, waterfalls, and confluence of Rio Grande and Frijoles Creek.

Solitude Rating: ★★★

How to get there: Take US 285/84 to Pojoaque, and then go west on NM 502. Turn south on NM 4 and continue to the entrance.

Accessibility from highway: Easy.

Facilities: Nearest gas is in White Rock or Los Alamos. Visitor center with snack bar, restrooms, and water. Camping available.

Fee Area: Yes.

*B*andelier, an impossible place to stay away from, is a powerful, enchanted place. (See the Shrine of the Stone Lions, page 141 and the Tsankawi Indian Ruins, page 143, two other sites in the Bandelier backcountry.) This magical place is named for Adolph Bandelier, a self-taught anthropologist and historian who traveled here in 1880. In 18 months he visited 166 ruins in New Mexico, Arizona, and Mexico. But when men from the Cochiti Pueblo guided him here to their ancestral homes, these were the lands he considered the "grandest."

You definitely want to visit Bandelier in the off-season, which means early spring, autumn, or winter. Spring and summer are the busiest times here, and you may have to wait more than half an hour just to park. Bummer, but you know the rules. If you must go during heavy times, go early—but don't expect much solitude.

When you arrive at the parking lot of Bandelier, the visitor center is right before you. You must pass through the visitor center to continue to the cliff dwellings. The trail is paved, and there's no place to go for solitude. If you're like me, you may quickly tire of all the signs that tell you what not to do. Surely there's a better way.

Regardless, persevere, as three places along this loop are truly inspirational. The first is a very rare sight, a cave kiva, a sacred place of religious ceremony and ceremonial weaving. You can still see the depressions on the floor where weavings were anchored.

A dazzling, burnt-orange pictograph below a cliff-side, tube-shaped cave also caught my fancy. Also home to a colony of Mexican freetailed bats, this is a power spot indeed. It must have been quite a scene when the group of 10,000 bats first arrived in 1986! They return every spring to give birth to their pups before migrating south for the winter. *Note:* Remember that caves are fragile and often dangerous environments; please exercise caution when visiting them.

From the main ruin's loop, you can either return to the visitor center or cross the stream, turn right, and continue to the ceremonial cave. This large natural shelter, which sits 140 feet above the canyon floor, is accessible by ladders. It's steep, and you need nonslip shoes, but you're rewarded with a remarkable rebuilt kiva—plus the opportunity to stand and feel this place of wonder that amplifies the smallest sounds. Your streamside return to the visitor center is glorious. The stream flows beside you as you meander through grand, old ponderosa pine estimated to be between 200 and 300 years old.

The next leg of your journey is less developed and will most likely be less peopled, too. An easy-to-moderate dirt trail, which is quite rocky in places, takes you about 5 miles from the top of the trailhead to the confluence of Frijoles Creek and the Rio Grande. Going in and down is easier than the return. Cross the creek at the visitor center, walk downstream through the backcountry parking lot, and you'll see the well-marked trail. It's 5 miles round-trip to the Rio Grande—and worth every step.

On the upper end of this trail you walk through magnificent forests of ponderosa pine, box elder, oak, and cottonwood. The trail offers many opportunities to break off and find quiet and beautiful places to sit. At about 1.5 miles, you come to Upper Falls, the first of two waterfalls on this hike. Lower Falls, a little farther down the trail, is potent and beautiful. Unfortunately, you must view them from a "safe" distance—the trails to the base are closed, and signs warn of great hazard. (Despite the warnings, the trails are well-worn.)

From the falls, you drop down to the streamside and continue to the Rio Grande. Walk amongst the deep canyon walls, where the lush earth abounds with flowers and healing plants such as the emerald-green, reedlike horsetail. The canyon is a geological wonder, with rocks and strata telling the stories of time. You'll feel the presence of the peoples who came before and lived on these lands, their stories held safely within the soft, swollen mud rock.

Stories carried away. Down, down, to the muddy Rio Grande. Where one bundle of tales meets another, in a magnificent dance of convergence.

37. Heron Lake

Heron Lake State Park
P.O. Box 159
Los Ojos, NM 87511
505-588-7470
www.emnrd.state.nm.us/nmparks/pages/heron/heron.htm

Location: 13 miles southwest of Chama.

Description: A serene, 5,900-acre lake at 7,200 feet on the boundary of the Jicarilla Apache lands. Powerboats operate at no-wake speeds only and sailboats and kayaks prevail. The land of Heron Lake State Park encompasses 4,100 acres.

Spiritual Significance: Called "the quiet lake," this is home to osprey and kokanee salmon.

Solitude Rating: ★★★★

How to get there: Heron Lake is 11 miles west of Tierra Amarilla on NM 95.

Accessibility from highway: Easy.

Facilities: Developed and undeveloped campgrounds; visitor center staffed by wonderfully seasoned individuals glad to see you and even more glad to help; camp bathrooms; picnic tables; sailing; lake kayaking. Food, gas, and boat rentals available several miles away.

Fee Area: Yes.

*I*t is not often that you have the opportunity to visit a wake-less lake, where wind and muscle set the tone. Heron Lake is one of these, offering the opportunity to be upon vast waters in the quiet and calm of natural wonders such as the Narrows, with the magnificent Brazos Cliffs in the distance. Primitive camping areas exist on the east and west ends of the lake at the first and last turnoffs within the park. Fully equipped sites for RVs are available throughout. As with all state parks, the use of generators is prohibited during quiet times (from 10 p.m. to 7 a.m.).

Set up camp and take in the splendor. More than 60 species of birds live in this area, including the regal osprey (or fish hawk). When I visited in late June, I witnessed a mother osprey on her nest with two fledglings. If you've never seen an osprey dive for fish, then you are in for a miraculous event. (*Note:* Osprey nests are easy to view, because they build their nests on top of trees or power poles. However, this leaves their chicks susceptible to the sun. Do not get so close as to scare the female from her eggs. It takes only a few minutes for the eggs or the young to get too warm and die.) Bald eagles winter here and rattlesnakes slither across the roads. You may see a black bear, mountain lion, or the fascinating Abert squirrel, all common totems of the spirit seeker.

Mild lake breezes make this lake the perfect place to set sail, physically or metaphorically. If you wish, you can arrange a day or overnight kayak trip with Kayak Kerr Company (505-588-9317). If walking in beauty is your pleasure, the Rio Chama Trail begins just east of the dam and continues 5.5 miles along the deep, Chama River canyon, through a forest full of lush habitat, birds, and wildlife. The trail eventually ends at another large lake, El Vado.

To many, the dazzling silence of cross-country skiing is sacred. To some, sacred is the feel of a kokanee salmon on the end of a fishing line. To others, it doesn't get more Zen than paddling across still, glassy waters. You can do all these at Heron Lake—or nothing at all.

38. Kasha-Katuwe Tent Rocks National Monument

BLM and Cochiti Pueblo
P.O. Box 70
Cochiti Pueblo, NM 87072
505-761-8700 (BLM) or 505-465-2244 (Pueblo)

Location: 40 miles southwest of Santa Fe
and 50 miles northeast of Albuquerque.

Description: Eroded rock pinnacles and a daring slot canyon
at approximately 6,000 feet.

Spiritual Significance: Geological power spot, ancestral Indian lands,
a place of wonder and magnificence.

Solitude Rating: ★★★★
(Others may be on the trail, but it's easy to find a private place to sit.)

How to get there: Take I-25 south of Santa Fe (north of Albuquerque)
to the Cochiti Pueblo/Reservoir exit 264. Turn onto NM 16. Go 8 miles to
a T-intersection, and then turn right onto NM 22, heading towards the
massive Cochiti Dam. NM 22 turns left at the base of the dam and heads
toward Cochiti Pueblo. Go 1.8 miles to the end of NM 22 and turn right
onto Tribal Route 92/FR 266. (Note the water towers painted like drums!)
It's another 5 miles on a dirt/gravel road—bumpy and dusty, but OK for
any vehicle. A parking area, the only one, is on the right.

Accessibility from highway: Fair.

Facilities: Picnic tables and bathrooms for day use only.
Far from gas and food.

Fee Area: Yes.

Kasha-Katuwe Tent Rocks National Monument is named for the tent (or
tipi) shape of the wind- and rain-carved pumice cones. The eroded spires
are an "in-spire-ation" and the slot canyon evokes mystery and wonder.

Don't undertake this journey on a whim. Call before you make the
long drive, as the monument can be closed for sacred tribal events. Be sure
to wear shoes or boots with good traction, and be prepared to do some
rock scrambling. Don't expect a lot of signs on the trail; the long trail is
one way in, one way out, with little guidance. Bring plenty of water and
wear a hat in summer (the earlier or later in the day you visit, the better).
Before you begin, check the weather report—and don't enter if major rains
are imminent.

At the parking lot, you will see a map of the area—begin walking
here. Up the trail a short ways, a trail breaks off to the left. The left spur is
a shorter, easier loop for sightseers. You can try this trail later if you wish,
but it does not offer the solitude and wonder of the longer trail. Continue

on the long trail, up the sandy wash. The trail soon narrows and you enter the dramatic slot canyon—this is where you want to be. The trail gets steeper as you continue, but the beauty never ceases as you squeeze and high-step and duck your way up the trail. You'll find many places off the trail where you can sit and ponder. On the upper end of the trail, you reach a height that offers views into the valleys and into the many pinnacles. This upper climb is a challenge, however, and not clearly marked.

In the bowels of Tent Rocks, once again, you are witness to the power of volcanism, a predominant theme of the New Mexico landscape. These lands were originally a 400-foot-deep sheath of volcanic material, slowly cut and formed by the forces of nature. The Rio Grande flows nearby, now captured and controlled by a humongous earthen dam built by the Army Corps of Engineers.

Tent Rocks is forever changing. Every gust of wind, every drop of rain, brings transformation. Look for Apache Tears in the sand: small, black, shiny rocks that resemble tears. Greenleaf manzanita bursts from the ground, and Apache Plume, a wispy, white-flowered shrub of the drylands, tickles the air. You are in a very extraordinary place.

39. Kit Carson Memorial Park Cemetery

Taos

This cemetery was born of the bloody Taos Revolt of 1847, when U.S. troops stormed the San Gerónimo de Taos Church on the Taos Pueblo to quell an Indian and Hispanic rebellion against the Anglo-American settlers. By the end of the three-week rebellion, hundreds were dead and the original San Gerónimo Church was reduced to what it is today, the target of cannon-balls and gunfire. Doña Teodora Martinez Romero donated this cemetery land, at the edge of Taos at the time, to bury the dead. Originally called El Cementerio Militia, the name was changed to the American Cemetery in 1852 and to Kit Carson Cemetery in 1869 (after Kit and Josepha Carson were buried here).

Tucked away in a corner of Kit Carson Park, this tiny cemetery is something special. The first thing you notice is the grave outside the fenced boundaries. This is the final resting place of Arthur Manby, a British aristocrat, who owned these lands at one time and lived in a huge hacienda that included the Stables Art Gallery. Kit Carson Park served as his personal gardens, filled with beautiful trees and bushes. He was the first to provide lodging for Mabel Dodge Luhan when she arrived in Taos. Trained as an architect, mineralogist, and painter, he was a less-than-ingenuous early

Location: In the heart of Taos.

Description: Final resting place for the famous and infamous, this camposanto (cemetery) is a treasure trove of New Mexico history.

Spiritual Significance: Resting place of the dead.

Solitude Rating: ★★★

How to get there: In Kit Carson Park, off Pueblo del Norte just north of the plaza stoplight.

Accessibility from highway: Easy.

Facilities: The town has almost everything.

Fee Area: No.

businessman in Taos and a land swindler extraordinaire. He made lots of enemies and was found beheaded on July 4, 1929.

Inside the wire cemetery fence you find the grave of Padre Martinez, the rebellious priest to whom many claim direct familial ties (at that time, it was not unusual for priests in New Mexico to have mistresses and to father children). Father Martinez brought the first printing press to New Mexico and made his way into politics. Many believe he had a clandestine role in the Taos Rebellion.

Mabel Dodge, salon mistress from Italy to New York, settled in Taos, married Tony Luhan, a Pueblo Indian, and became a prominent citizen, benefactress, and philanthropist (see Mabel Dodge Luhan House Inn and Retreat, page 95). She's buried here, back in the far corner, next to Ralph Meyers, a painter and Indian Trader popular with Taoseños (people who live in Taos). Yes, spirits run thick and wild here, from Kit Carson and his third wife Josepha Jaramillo (who died in childbirth), to Carson's personal, confidential secretary, to prominent Taos merchants who set up business on the Taos Plaza when it consisted of dirt and horses. The families of the Dolans, Lieberts, and Gusdorfs you see represented here are still active in the Taos business community today.

This cemetery encapsulates the history of New Mexico, and the Native American, Hispanic, and Anglo cultures make these lands as rich and fascinating today as they were throughout history. Many of the people buried here have riveting stories that followed them to their graves. Courageous and crazy, hardworking and stubborn, lonely and creative. Ravens beckon to the past as you stroll these gravel paths of olden-day Taos and ask yourself, "What stories will follow me?"

40. La Vista Verde Trail, Rio Grande Gorge

BLM Orilla Verde Recreation Area
Rio Grande Gorge Visitor Center
State Road 570 and NM 68
Pilar, NM 87531
505-751-4899

The La Vista Verde Trail is a short (1.25 miles, one way), easy, relatively level trail along a Rio Grande Gorge plateau. The 45- to 60-minute walk takes you to a lookout point over the Rio Grande Gorge. Your reward is a concrete bench on which to sit and ponder the universe. However, a few more steps take you to the "point," where you can sit on the ground in wonderment of the scene before you. The Rio Grande Gorge was created by tectonic plates and volcanic uplift—something to consider as you gaze upon the "Great River." The Rio begins in Colorado near Silverton, entering New Mexico at Ute Peak, the large, round mound of mountain to the north of Taos.

A marvelous aspect of this site is just getting to it. The drive from Pilar along the Rio Grande River is a sumptuous feast for the spirit, offering many picnic spots with tables where you can stop and dip your toe (or more) in

Location: South of Taos near the confluence of the Rio Pueblo and the Rio Grande.

Description: A marvelous hike with many scenic overlooks along the Rio Grande Gorge.

Spiritual Significance: River, confluence, rock, petroglyphs.

Solitude Rating: ★★★★

How to get there: On NM 68, head south from Taos for 16 miles to Pilar. At Pilar, turn right onto NM 570. Follow 570 for 6 miles along the Rio Grande, cross the bridge (the road becomes gravel at this point), and head up the steep, canyon-side road to the first major turnoff and sign designating the parking area for La Vista Verde Trail.

Accessibility from highway: Fair.

Facilities: None. Gas up and use the restroom before your turn off NM 68.

Fee Area: Yes.

the Rio's waters. The stretch from Pilar to the bridge is paved—a grand bike ride for those so inclined. Up the canyonside, the turnoff is not well-marked, but the trailhead is. Sneakers will be OK for this hike, but I prefer leather, well-constructed, low-cut boots for the rocky terrain and potential cactus spines. (Note that two other side trails will take you down to the river, but they're steep and rocky, requiring footwear with a good grip.)

What a hike this is! First, it's easy. Second, it's well-marked and full of fun, fascinating surprises. As you begin, watch for impromptu rock geoglyphs along the trail. Within your first few steps, the smell of sage overtakes you, and the splendid large rocks and the vastness of the gorge open your heart. As you walk, keep your eye out for some of the oldest petroglyphs found in the area. Look for geometric designs believed to be around 5,000 years old, along with handprints and masks that are 500 to 600 years old.

One of the best things about this hike is the many opportunities to easily wander off the trail. It's only a few steps to the gorge rim, where you can find peaceful, undisturbed places. Or, you can continue to the end of the trail and view the gorge and the magnificent Rio Grande, which was once called the Rio Bravo del Norte, the "Bold River of the North." I would suggest you do both. You will have no problem finding a place of quiet contemplation. Close your eyes and leave linear time behind, as ravens drift and "kraaaak" from the rock cliffs below. Canyon wrens cast their unmistakable trill from above. And the river, like time, just keeps flowing.

Note: The confluence of the Rio Pueblo and the Rio Grande—an ideal spot—is easily accessible. Rather than crossing the bridge and heading uphill to the parking area, continue straight, park, and walk one of the many trails to your left. The Rio Pueblo begins at the sacred Blue Lake, high in the Sangre de Cristo Mountains on the Taos Pueblo lands.

41. Petroglyph National Monument, Rinconada Canyon

Petroglyph National Monument
6001 Unser Boulevard, NW
Albuquerque, NM 87120
505-899-0205
www.nps.gov/petr

I almost skipped this area because it's in the city and I thought it might be too crowded and touristy. That would have been a mistake—a very big mistake. Once you enter Rinconada Canyon, you step more and more deeply into a special time before the arrival of the Anglos, when nature and mystery were predominate, and ritual the bridge between them. According to one theory, the villages below along the Rio Grande sent select people on spiritual missions to carve the petroglyphs in this escarpment. We will never know the who and why of their artistic record. We are left, instead, with their awesome drawings and a great test for our imaginations.

The hike is 2.5 to 3 miles round-trip and moderately strenuous, especially in the summer, when it can get very hot. The best spot to turn around is at the head of the canyon, when the route turns south

Location: On the far west side of Albuquerque.

Description: One of the most extensive and fascinating arrays of petroglyphs —there are more than 20,000—along a 17-mile escarpment, dating from 3,000 years ago.

Spiritual Significance: Petroglyphs, volcanic landscape, ancient Indian destination, sacred landscape to today's pueblo people.

Solitude Rating: ★★★

How to get there: Take I-40 to Exit 154, Unser Blvd. Continue north to the Rinconada Canyon turnoff on your left. (The visitor center is a short drive beyond this turnoff.)

Accessibility from highway: Easy.

Facilities: Restrooms at trailhead, everything else in the city.

Fee Area: No.

and petroglyphs become scarce. Wear protective footwear, take water (especially in the summer), and wear a hat. With no trees on this hike, the sun is unforgiving. Go early in the morning or go in the spring, fall, or winter.

The walk begins in the most uninspiring way: the sky is filled with a huge power line, the landscape is rocky and sparse, the sounds of traffic wander into your ears, and you wonder what the heck you're doing here. But then you pass beyond the high lines, and the traffic subsides out of earshot. Peace settles in as you see the images that give your walk purpose. And what a display it is—figures, spirals, masks, and macaws. Ninety percent of the petroglyphs are Indian. Hispanic crosses are pecked next to Indian figures, believed to nullify the pagan spirit. The petroglyphs stretch across rock after rock, sometimes making their way around the sharp stone edges to become two-sided. Handprints, deer, and what looks like a giant bear paw are among the oh-so-many images that have no name, destined to enter our imaginations and create their own stories.

If you're staying at an Albuquerque retreat, this trail is the perfect outing. Even if you're just passing through, stop. Miles of backcountry hiking in Colorado and New Mexico will rarely be rewarded with a spectacle such as this easily accessible display in the canyon called Rinconada—a place held sacred today by Pueblo Indians.

42. San Antonio Mountain

North of Tres Piedras

San Antonio Mountain lies formidably upon the earth. Years ago, I dubbed her "Mound Calm" as I meditated on her from my cabin 100 miles to her north. San Antonio was named for Saint Anthony, the founder of the Desert Monastics, the Father of Monks. Anyone who sees and feels the presence of this mountain, however, knows that her likeness is the penultimate breast of the earth. The Tewa Indians consider her to be a *Tsin*, one of four sacred hills where important spirits are believed to live. San Antonio is their northern boundary; their names for her mean "Bear Mountain."

Come here and you will find silence. Come here and your feet join the hooves of pronghorn antelope and elk, your ears hear the song of the meadowlark, and your skin tingles with the vast openness of the high-mountain desert as the smell of sage envelopes your soul.

Location: 10 miles south of the Colorado border, north of Tres Piedras.

Description: Located in the high-desert terrain of the San Luis Valley, this is the highest freestanding mountain in the continental United States (the altitude is 7,000 feet at the base and 10,908 feet at the top). Overlapping lava flows formed the shield volcano.

Spiritual Significance: Volcano, mountain, sacred hill of the Tewa.

Solitude Rating: ★★★★★

How to get there: Take US 285 north from Santa Fe or south from Colorado. The mountain stands mighty and alone, 10 miles south of the Colorado border.

Accessibility from highway: Easy to fair.

Facilities: None. Gas up in Tres Piedras or Antonito, Colo., before you turn off the highway.

Fee Area: No.

US 285 shoots right by the east side of San Antonio Mountain, as do most cars on their way to Santa Fe or Denver. From the highway you see a small pullout, which announces the presence of the mountain, and a small, misguided subdivision that sprouted on the mountain's east face.

North and south of the mountain, however, a gravel road heads west, embracing the mountain in a horseshoe configuration. From the north, take Forest Road 118. From the south, it's Forest Road 87. The road numbers change halfway around the mountain, at an intersection at the 7-mile point. (The entire horseshoe runs approximately 14 miles.) It's slow going on the two-track gravel road around San Antonio Mountain. But then, driving slow is part of the adventure as you stop to watch a diving kestrel or a bounding pronghorn antelope. The northern entrance has a rough, rutted beginning, but levels out after about 3 miles. The road condition, of course, is subject to change. But the higher clearance your vehicle has, the easier time you will have.

Once you begin your drive around "Antonia," you move out of Bureau of Land Management (BLM) designation and rules and into Carson National Forest. This means that, except for the small development on the east side of the mountain, the mountain is public land—yours. The primary rule for both the BLM and Carson National Forest is to stay on marked roads and paths. You can easily pull off and camp to within 300 feet of the road, or park your vehicle and head for the aspen and pine/fir forests and various springs just a mile up the mountain. An easy backpack up old roads brings you to undeveloped, mountainside campsites of solitude, beauty and vast views. A short, strenuous hike takes you to the mountaintop. (Hike from the western side of the mountain so you will be well away from the transmitter for a public radio station in Alamosa, Colo.) If you prefer to car-camp at the base of the mountain, a grassy spot with several fire rings gives you a beautiful view of the mountain, but finding solitude is chancier. To reach this camping area, turn west at the intersection on the west side of the mountain. Don't worry about missing the intersection—there's only one!

This mountain offers incredible opportunities for spiritual solitude for those who are willing to leave the comforts of modern living behind, put their lives on their backs, and join the elk at high altitude. From the top, you view desert, canyon, volcanic cones, and plateau upon plateau. The magnificent mountain you see to the northeast is Blanca Peak, or Tsisnaajini, the Navajo sacred mountain of the east. To Blanca Peak's left, the Great Sand Dunes and the awesome spine of the Sangre de Cristos sprawl. (See *Colorado's Sanctuaries, Retreats, and Sacred Places,* another book in this series; in this book, see Tsoodzil, page 54, for a description of the Navajo sacred mountain of the south.)

If mountaintops are not your cup of tea, there are miles and miles of developed and undeveloped public lands and roads in the area, along which you are sure to find a spot for contemplation—unless it is hunting season in autumn. Check on hunting season dates to ensure safety and quiet.

43. Shrine of the Stone Lions

Bandelier National Monument
HCR I, Box 1, Suite 15
Los Alamos, NM 87544
505-672-0343 or 505-672-3861

I didn't know the stone lions were here the first time I came upon them, which was like entering a strange and mysterious world, the likes of which I have never experienced. Even the unexcavated ruins of Yapashi, less than a mile before, had not prepared me for the beautiful and simple Shrine of the Stone Lions. A place of primitive, raw power.

You reach the Shrine on the Yapashi Trail, a bold and beautiful path through the rugged Alamo Canyon, a jaunt that turns the journey into a pilgrimage you won't soon forget. First you drop 600 feet into the canyon with its lush riparian bottomlands, and then you climb out again, a hike that demands every bit of willpower. Approximately 5 miles from the beginning you reach the unexcavated ruins of Yapashi, an ancient Cochiti Pueblo ruin, whose name means "circle of rocks." Approximately 200 people occupied this place from A.D. 1325 to 1450. Here, you feel the spirits of

Location: North of Santa Fe in Bandelier National Monument.

Description: Strenuous, 12-mile round-trip hike through forests, meadows, and steep canyons to the ancient village of Yapashi, a remote archeological site, and to the awe-inspiring Shrine of the Stone Lions.

Spiritual Significance: Unexcavated pueblo, ancient hunting shrine.

Solitude Rating: ★★★★★

How to get there: From the Los Alamos exit on US 285/84, go west on NM 502. Turn onto NM 4, to White Rock and follow the signs to Bandelier. Stop at the park headquarters to receive your free backcountry permit, instructions, and maps. From this location, you will hike the Mesa Rim Trail, which connects to the Yapashi Trail after about 1 mile. Carry all the food, water, and backpacking gear you will need. A day hike is at least 8 hours of constant hiking at a good pace.

Accessibility from highway: Remote and difficult.

Facilities: None, once you leave the visitor center, which has bathrooms, water, and concessions.

Fee Area: Yes.

the descendants. Here, you see their pottery shards and walk in their footsteps. Remember to leave everything where you find it, in full respect to the Native American families for whom ruins are sacred sanctuaries for the spirits of the Pueblo underworld.

Continue down the path, less than a mile, to the Shrine of the Stone Lions. First you will see a ring of large rocks about 20 feet in diameter. In the middle of the ring are two elongated, stone mountain lions, carved from volcanic rock. Early people revered cougars, still inhabitants of these lands, for many reasons. The powerful, swift animals with beautiful balance are stealthy hunters, who waste no steps. Cougars mark their home range with scrapes (a scratch in the soil marked with claws, feces, or urine), and they respect the territories of other lions. A person with "cougar qualities" was sure of his or her purpose in life, preferred solitude, and didn't think twice about taking the easiest prey.

Sit with the all-powerful spirits of this place. This is a deeply sacred site to the Pueblo peoples, who continue to visit and hold ceremony. You will, perhaps, never find a more holy space to pray and ponder. These carvings of such a strong animal are so unique. If it is puma energy you seek, it crouches before you.

Leave the lions in untouched peace. The native peoples ask that we do not leave offerings and that the shrine remain free of any signs of visitation. As with most sites, leave only prayers.

44. Tsankawi Indian Ruins

Bandelier National Monument
HCR I, Box 1, Suite 15
Los Alamos, NM 87544
505-672-0343 or 505-672-3861

Tsankawi is where you go to walk in the steps of the Old Ones. Literally. The steps and stairs of prehistoric peoples have worn and cut, over time, into the soft volcanic stone. In some places, the trail cuts into the rock more than a foot deep. Take water with you on this walk, and be sure to wear soft-soled, good-grip shoes along with clothes you can move in to navigate the two ladders on this trail. You may see people in the parking lot and on the trail, but there are many private spots in which to sit and take in the energy of this mystical spot. The earlier or later, the better—the evening light is incredible.

I love this trail. It demands involvement with the landscape, as you softly tread the trails of the early Anasazi. The path leads up through deeply cut stone, setting the imagination free to wonder and wander.

Once on top of the Pajarito "Little Bird" Plateau, you find yourself in the midst of the remains of a 350-room pueblo, with a magnificent view of the Rio Grande Valley. To the Tiwa Indians, *Tsankawi* means "village between two canyons at the clump of sharp, round cacti." Here, you see the Española Valley and the Sangre de Cristo Mountains to the east. To the south are the Sandia Mountains, east of Albuquerque. *Sandía* is Spanish for "watermelon," but the range is named more, perhaps, for the striped, red appearance of the rock and its pulpy texture than for melons grown there. The Tiwa Indians called their village to the south *Na-fi-at,* meaning "dusty place." Melons don't do well in dust, but they do very well in the sand, which lined the banks of the Rio Grande. Look south, into the Sandias, and let your imagination fly. The Sandia Mountains, sacred to the Tiwa, marked the southern boundary of their world. This mesa is covered with pottery shards— more remembrances of the peoples who called this home.

The trail leads from the mesa top to a ladder that takes you to the final leg of the loop. This final descent drops you into the cliff-side cave dwellings. It is amazing to think that these caves were once smoothly plastered, with roof beams and household fires. These rooms

Location: 12 miles north of Bandelier National Monument.

Description: A fascinating, 1.5 mile round-trip, loop trail to the Tsankawi Pueblo, built around A.D. 1400 at 6,600 feet elevation.

Spiritual Significance: Mesa-top Indian ruins, petroglyphs, caves.

Solitude Rating: ★★★★

How to get there: Although part of Bandelier National Monument, Tsankawi is a detached unit, about 12 miles from the main park. Take NM 502 to NM 4, and then go about 1 mile to the parking lot on your left.

Accessibility from highway: Easy.

Facilities: Covered picnic tables, trash receptacles, toilets, and drinking water. Gas and lodging in nearby White Rock and Los Alamos. Day use only, dawn to dusk. No pets allowed on the trail.

Fee Area: No.

and caves faced south to take full advantage of winter sun. Note the footstep ladders that climb the cliff. Here, you can sit and ride the glide of a raven's wing. Here, you can actually *see* canyon wrens fill the fissures with their unmistakable trill.

The remainder of the ledge trail—well-marked and fairly level— passes by many petroglyphs and is perfect for a dreamy walk.

Other Sacred Places

Coronado State Monument, Bernalillo, 505-867-5351

Puye Cliff Dwellings, Santa Clara Pueblo, 505-753-7326

Spiritual Events

45. Cambalache

Around October 1, Questa

Cambalache is Spanish for "swap" or "trade." And so it is in the Hispanic village of Questa, about 20 miles north of Taos, during its yearly trade fair. One of many *festivals de otoño* (autumn festivals) across the New Mexico countryside, this celebration is full of crops of the fields, fruits of the trees, and arts of the hand. Much more than booths, however, the event draws out villagers who show up to trade smiles, friendship, and news. The music is gay, the dancing fun, and the art a wonderful representation of the landscape.

As the festival day dies down, preparation begins for the burning of *el cucui,* the traditional bogeyman across Hispanic cultures. *El cucui, el kookooee,* coco man…whatever the name, he has come through the ages to scare kids into behaving. One Albuquerque woman describes the *el coco* of her childhood as a coyotelike figure who carried a whip for bad children. No matter the form he takes, the story is the same: If you don't obey, he is the bad guy who takes you away forever.

The head of the bogeyman effigy is stuffed with paper notes, called *penas*, the written worries of the people. To the cheers of the small, home-town crowd, *el cucui* is lit, and with it the fears and apprehensions of the villagers turn into smoke amidst the bounty and breezes.

Come fill your bags with the sacred bounty of the earth—local honey, jams and jellies, produce, baked and canned goods, eggs, medicinal herbs, melons, and yummy yeast breads. This intimate festival, rich in history and folklore, delights and "frights."

Cambalache is held in early October from 9 a.m. to 5:30 p.m. at the Artesanos de Questa Cultural Center, next to the post office in Questa on NM 38 (the road to Red River). Call the cultural center at 505-586-0443 for details.

46. Las Posadas

December 16–December 24
St. Francis de Asis Church
Ranchos de Taos

*T*his touching reenactment of Maria and José's (Mary and Joseph's) search for shelter in Bethlehem on Christmas Eve lasts for nine nights, beginning with a 6 p.m. Mass on December 16 and continuing nightly until Christmas Eve. Mass is followed by a processional, led by a diminutive Virgin Maria, that all are invited to join. In many reenactments across the state of New Mexico, Virgin Maria is perched upon the back of the burro, led by San José. A candlelight procession includes children dressed as angels, the Three Kings, and *pastores y pastoras* (shepherds and shepherdesses). Urged on by the impending birth of the Christ Child, they walk to a house, where José pleads for a place to spend the night through a *posada* (lodging) song in Spanish, which is a dialogue in which José beseeches the innkeeper not to be inhumane and to let them in. Maria and José are turned away in a very moving exchange, and the procession moves to the next house. After several exchanges, José announces that his wife is Maria, Queen of the Heavens, soon to give birth. On the final evening, December 24, the innkeeper receives them and everyone enters the house in celebration and joy.

Each Las Posadas takes on its own personality, reflecting the community in which it is held. If you are in New Mexico this time of year, check to see if there is a Las Posadas in the town you are visiting. Sometimes it is a one-night event, but often it is a nine-evening ritual. This Las Posadas rotates between the main church and the small mission chapels; call 505-758-2754 for details.

El Rito Shrine for Nuestra Señora northeast of Abiquiu.

47. Mass Ascension, Hot-Air Balloon Fiesta

Beginning of October, Albuquerque

The sight of a hot-air balloon drifting above ground is a wondrous reminder of our proximity to heaven. With its lift go our worries. On its breeze-carried trail travels our imagination. If one balloon has such a lofty effect on our souls, imagine the effect of hundreds of hot air balloons. The spectacle is unbelievable—a sky literally filled with gigantic shapes, a kaleidoscope of colors, and flames from the burners. The sight is like nothing else, which is why the annual Kodak Albuquerque International Balloon Fiesta has become *the* hot air-ballooning event in the world. It's also the largest, with pilots and balloons from across the globe.

Every morning features a mass ascension at 7 a.m., when you will see several hundred balloons lift off and fill the sky in unison. Themes for the mass ascensions include Flight of Nations and Special Shapes. Look up

The mass ascension at the International Hot-Air Balloon Fiesta in Albuquerque. Photo by William Stone.

during the Special Shapes ascension, sure to delight the child in all of us, and see a pink piggy bank with a red roof over its head, an elephant, exotic birds from Brazil, a smiling airplane named Jumbo Jim, and a devilish-looking balloon called Cuddles. The Wells Fargo stagecoach balloon is nearly four times larger than the average balloon, the teeny human-filled basket hanging from beneath its four, large-spoked wheels. And who says pigs can't fly?

Sundown balloon glows are yet another marvel to rouse the soul. Eerily otherworldly, they are an event of unmatched beauty. At 5:30 p.m., you stand in wait for the signal that will flame and light hundreds of tethered balloons simultaneously, producing a dream of billowing, phantasmic color and light.

If spectacle is the food of the soul, then this event is a veritable feast. There is nothing like a hot-air balloon to cast us once again as children. With this autumnal fiesta of balloons comes a special kind of innocence, a return to simpler times, when winds and weather ruled the skies and earth.

The Kodak Albuquerque International Balloon Fiesta takes place in the beginning of October for one week. Make motel reservations months in advance. Once in town, pick up a copy of the *Albuquerque Journal* special balloon fiesta supplement. Find one of the several park-and-ride pickup spots around the city or park at the Fiesta for a fee. The Fiesta is on the north end of Albuquerque. If you drive, exit Tramway from I-25, and proceed west. Gates open at 4:30 a.m. for morning events and at 3 p.m. for the evening events. For information, call the Albuquerque Convention and Visitor Bureau at 505-842-9918 or the balloon fiesta offices at 888-422-7277.

A much smaller balloon fiesta takes place in the center of Taos toward the end of October. Call the Taos Chamber of Commerce at 505-758-3873 or 800-732-TAOS (8267) for details. What it lacks in spectacle, it makes up for in intimacy.

48. Procession of the Virgin

Dusk, December 24
Taos Pueblo

Throughout New Mexico, the Christmas season abounds with sacred festivities. From precious Las Posadas, the Hispanic Christmas Eve reenactment of Mary and Joseph's search for a shelter, to the lighting of *luminarias* and *farolitas* in town plazas and side streets, you will be hard-pressed to find more beautiful and authentic presentations this holy time of year. Of all the holiday celebrations I've experienced, none is as breathtaking as the Christmas Eve procession of the Virgin at the Taos Pueblo.

You arrive at the end of the day, as the sun eases down behind the tiny San Gerónimo Chapel. The sky streaks tangerine and lavender as the vespers begin inside and crowds gather outside, milling in solemn wait. Towering fires of pitch wood are lit, casting shadows and smoke. As darkness falls, the church bells begin to ring, announcing the procession of the Madonna. The wooden church doors open as men carry her beautiful, veiled figure into the night, where men carrying torches and playing drums join her. A line of protectors with rifles fires their guns to keep evil away and to ensure her safe advance. Winds gust, as the heaps of piñon and ponderosa pine surge into flaming infernos. Drumbeat, gunfire and chants fill the air, as children cringe and adults look in awe upon this powerful drama of auspicious spectacle.

The Taos Pueblo is north of Taos. From the downtown plaza, drive north on US 64 until you come to a well-marked, paved road that branches off to your right (follow the signs for the Taos Casino). Call 505-758-1028 or 505-758-9593 for information.

49. Saint Francis of Assisi Feast Day

October 3–4
Nambe Pueblo

The Nambe Pueblo hugs the Sangre de Cristo Mountains, just south of Chimayo. A powerful place of beauty, it is home to the pueblo whose feast-day dance is one of the most colorful you will see anywhere. *Nambe* means "people of the round earth." Not far from the pueblo, on the south side of the Rio Nambe, sit adobe round-earth mounds, remains of the ancient village. As caretakers of the earth, the people of Nambe carry a deep responsibility to their ancestors to maintain tradition and pass it on to their children. You will see this responsibility in action on their Feast Day of Saint Francis.

The celebration begins the evening of October 3 with vespers, an evening dance, fires, and a shower of treats. Festivities resume at sunrise the following morning, when another service is held in the church mid-morning, followed by a processional of people carrying various *santos* around the village. Not long after the processional, the dancing begins with dazzling steps and a spectacle of color, sound, and motion. Mystery and power emanate from the men's faces, painted in patterns of stripes divided into halves. The women are exquisite in their bright colors, comely high white moccasins, and dots upon their cheeks. All the dancers—men, women and children—proceed around the plaza, sprinkling cornmeal upon the sacred rock-lined shrine, not far from the mighty adobe kiva. On the day I attended, the dance was filled with the energy of the eagle, as the adorned dancers carried and wore more sacred feathers than I have seen in any other dance.

The Nambe Pueblo is located 20 miles north of Santa Fe, 18 miles east of Española on Road 101. For information, call 505-455-2036 before October 3.

50. San Gerónimo Day

September 29–30, Taos Pueblo

The Taos Pueblo stands proudly and beautifully below Taos Mountain. Built of adobe, it is the largest surviving multistoried Pueblo structure in the United States and is a World Heritage Site, in good company with the Taj Mahal, the Great Pyramids, and the Grand Canyon. San Gerónimo Day is the largest event of the year, a sacred, fascinating, fun, and wonderful time that includes a traditional footrace, an all-day trade fair, intertribal dancing, and a pole climb. You know you are in for something very special when you enter the plaza of the pueblo and see the towering, smooth-shaven pine tree trunk looming above you. And hanging from its top are the fruits of the harvest, including squash, rounds of fry bread, and a sheep with its throat cut.

Ceremonies open to the public begin with vespers on the evening of Sept. 29 around 5 p.m. The footraces begin early the next morning, around 8 a.m. A relay race of barefooted men, this event takes you back to a time long past. The men materialize from two distant kivas, painted and adorned with grasses tied around their necks. Dressed only in loincloths, they await their turns to run the long, dirt path to the next runners in the

The crosses marking this Penitente *morada* manifest the brotherhood's religious faith and ascetic lifestyle.

relay. Old, old men. Little, tiny ones. And every age in between. Lining the runway are Pueblo women adorned in their colorful, fringed shawls and traditional, white princess boots. You get the feeling they have watched these men race from childhood to old age in this ritual that defies time. Spend your day on the pueblo visiting the houses whose owners welcome you in to see their beautiful, handcrafted wares for sale. Or, visit the many booths that sell jewelry, food, furniture, and clothing. The day leads up to the pole climb, but not before the clowns make their appearance and their presence known through outrageous acts of mimicry, teasing, and fun. Don't be offended if they jiggle your dignity as they work the periphery of the crowd, moving toward the center and the pole they attempt to climb. The drama is great, as one makes it all the way to the top amidst the applause and awe of the crowd. And this is only the beginning of a mysterious and exciting happening. Note that pole climbs are one of those rare Pueblo events in which the crowds are encouraged to applaud.

The Taos Pueblo is north of the Taos. From the downtown plaza, drive north on US 64 until you come to a well-marked, paved road that branches off to your right (follow the signs for the Taos Casino). Call 505-758-1028 or 505-758-9593 for information.

A roadside sign shows spiritual travelers the way.

51. San Lorenzo Feast Day

August 9–10, Picuris Pueblo

The tiny Picuris Pueblo lies off the beaten path, high within the Sangre de Cristo Mountains. Coronado's expedition missed it completely when they explored the area in 1540. The Picuris, like their Taos Pueblo neighbors to the northwest, are Northern Tiwa. Their pueblo once consisted of great adobe structures, believed to have been up to eight stories high. Once one of the largest pueblos, the Picuris Pueblo now numbers fewer than 300 inhabitants.

The intimate San Lorenzo Feast Day takes place on the anniversary of the Pueblo revolt of 1680. The ceremony begins on August 9 with sunset vespers at the awe-inspiring San Lorenzo de Picuris Catholic Church, built in the 1770s. The second day, August 10, includes traditional foot races, ceremonial dances, and the pole climb. As you walk down the hill into the central plaza, you see the pole standing straight and high with its bounty secured at the top—a sheep, a watermelon, and a colorful cloth. San Lorenzo's shrine stands opposite the pole, across the plaza, towards the church. This simple, bough-laden structure is adorned with a beautiful star quilt. Be sure to visit the church as well as the unusual, ancient tower kiva at the ruins of Old Picuris. Many food and craft booths are here for your pleasure.

In mid-afternoon, the dancers appear to the beat of the drum and bells and rattles. The group is small and ever so intent. Your heart opens as you sink into the poetic beat held constant by the old men and the women's modest, princess-boot steps. And then you see them, far off, way across the plaza and up the hill, on a rooftop. Nine clowns, yucking it up and wreaking havoc, as the dancers keep beat to their drum. These clowns are *the* best! Down they come, teasing the dancers and rousing the crowd. You are subject to a long and wonderful show. And then you realize—the clowns will be the ones to climb the towering pine. "You are born into this clan," confided the Picuris woman who sat next to me, referring to the clowns. They are not assigned because they are good at climbing. Some years they must use the ladder to give the climber a head start. This year, to the claps and cheers of community and crowd, the clown made it on his own!

Note: Yes, it can be confusing—normally the crowd does not clap and cheer at ceremonial events. But if you are signaled to do so by the clowns or Pueblo participants, join in!

The Picuris Pueblo is on NM 75, 23 miles south of Taos, 55 miles north of Santa Fe. Call 505-587-2519 for information.

52. Santo Domingo Feast Day and Green Corn Dance

August 4, Santo Domingo Pueblo

This is the day that the Santo Domingo Pueblo honors their patron saint, St. Dominic. As you enter the parking area, the first thing you see is a county fair–like celebration of food booths, carnival rides, and cotton candy. But if you listen, you will hear the drumbeats. And if you follow the drumbeats into the pueblo plaza, you will bear witness to a spectacle of more than a thousand dancers filling the skies with the sounds of rattles and bells and song as they move to the beats of their sacred corn dance.

The corn dance—sometimes called the *tablita* dance for the wooden *tablitas* (small boards) on the women's heads—is a ripening ceremony and a deep plea for rain clouds to form and weep upon the hallowed corn. Everything you see and hear and smell beckons harmony and sustenance. Gourd rattles lure rain. Spruce boughs are endowed with the power to bring rain and heighten fertility. The painted bodies, off-the-shoulder dresses, silver and turquoise jewelry, pine branches worn on the body and methodically waved up and down, up and down—the beauty and power of it all mesmerize you as they summon the holy.

Corn dances, held every season throughout New Mexico's Native American lands, are all similar, yet different. Each embraces its own sense of mystery and beauty. But nowhere will you see the phenomenon and scale of this dance at Santo Domingo, as thousands of men, women, and children of all ages fill the sacred plaza with the prayer of dance.

Exit I-25 between Santa Fe and Albuquerque at the Santo Domingo exit. Take folding chairs and sun protection. No fee, but donations are appreciated. Observe pueblo etiquette, including absolutely no cameras (see How to Behave, page 21). Call 505-465-2214 for specifics.

53. Zia Pueblo Feast Day

August 15, Zia Pueblo

*M*any people have not heard of the Zia Pueblo—and those who have heard of it, may not have been there. You hardly notice it as you drive down the highway, as it sits camouflaged above you on a rocky, dry mesa top. Once 6,000-people strong, the pueblo population today is made up of about 700 industrious, proud people. The Zia's ancient sun symbol appears on the New Mexico State flag, their symbol for "perfect friendship among united cultures." And this is what you feel when you visit the Zia Pueblo on their Feast Day of Our Lady of the Assumption.

To attend this feast day and corn dance is to experience a truly special and holy event. Come early and walk through this small, splendid pueblo. Visit the booths of handmade jewelry and shawls. Ask to enter the bough-covered shrine to Our Lady of the Assumption on the far end of the plaza. Our Lady presides over the altar, where you can place your gift of money or tobacco. Visit the tiny church, perched on the highest mesa point, its altar heaped with baskets of fruit, vegetables, and baked goods.

Many people put their chairs along the church grounds, adjacent to the flat dancing area below. This is where the corn dancers come first, in the late morning. They then move to the central plaza—all ages creating a collage of drumbeat and pine bough and long black hair, waving from waist to thigh. The costumes are stunning. Note the large, red spots painted on the women's cheeks, the earthen zigzags and stripes on the men's hands. The men dance with exquisite high steps as the women's bare feet move across the sun-scorched ground. Rattles, bells, singers, and drums. Candles, handed to the dancers by women who do not dance, are carried into Our Lady's shrine.

The sun beats down and the dancing goes on and on, as the sacred corn grows higher and higher.

The Zia Pueblo is on US 550/NM 44, 18 miles northwest of Bernalillo. Call 505-867-3304 for information.

54. Zozobra

First Thursday after Labor Day, Santa Fe

The ritual burning of Old Man Gloom, also known as Zozobra, is an annual happening dear to Santa Fe. "Burn him! Burn him!" scream the thousands who come to cheer his demise. It's a primitive spectacle. The toothless, hideous-looking, 50-foot bogeyman is a metaphor for those parts of ourselves we want to get rid of. He has no guts (courage) and can't stand on his own two legs (he's a marionette). The annual rite, which kicks off the Fiesta de Santa Fe, is a symbolic community "offing" of the previous year's unhappiness. With his fiery purge, everyone starts afresh and pours into the streets to begin the celebrations of the fiesta, which has taken place since 1712.

Zozobra (pronounced so-so-bra) has been a part of the festivities since 1926. His construction takes place in two weeks, with more than a thousand hours of hard work by volunteers. On the Thursday night before the fiesta weekend, people begin their pilgrimage to Fort Marcy Park. They come early, with blankets and picnic baskets, to await the night and the fiery man who will ignite Zozobra. Finally he appears, as the giddy audience claps and screams, "Burn him!" The task is not hard—the torch spreads fire easily to the ghastly marionette stuffed with 80-plus garbage bags of shredded paper. Flames climb through his body, his arms wave, and a man with a microphone simulates his loud moans and groans. And the crowd is ecstatic—they laugh and cheer as they continue to chant, "Burn him, burn him!"

And so ends the gloom of the previous year. The fiesta, which originated in honor of La Conquistadora (see page 68 for information about her shrine) continues from Thursday night through Sunday, with streets full of mariachis, dancers, arts and crafts, green chile burritos and Indian fry bread, and even a children's pet parade. The fiesta is highlighted by a queen, marching priests, helmeted conquistadors, and solemn Mass and processions...but it begins with Zozobra.

The Fiesta de Santa Fe takes place the weekend after Labor Day. The burning of Zozobra takes place the Thursday night before the fiesta at Fort Marcy Park, a 15-minute walk north from the plaza. Gates open at 3 p.m.; the burning begins at nightfall. The event is staged by the Kiwanis Club, to whom Zozobra's originator, Will Shuster, assigned all rights. Visitors are encouraged to purchase discounted tickets in advance; visit www.zozobra.com.

Opposite: A statue depicting the namesake saint at San Francisco de Asis Church in Ranchos de Taos.

Region Three

Northeast:
The Windswept Corner

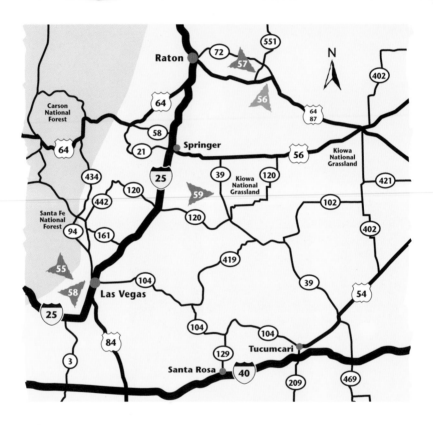

Sanctuaries

55. **Dwan Light Sanctuary** ....page 160

Retreats

56. **Mandala Center** 162
Other Retreats 163

Sacred Places

57. **Capulin Volcano National Monument** 164
58. **Hermit Peak** 166
59. **Mills Canyon** 169

This part of the state, more than any other, has the potential to give you the feeling of being the only person for miles around. This region begins in the hills east of the Sangre de Cristo Mountains and continues to the eastern state border. Here you travel rolling plains and grasslands amidst haunting, stark volcanic fields. Here, you can easily get off the main highways and travel for hours across country on gravel roads, through olden prairie settlements of early history. The Santa Fe Trail crossed this expanse, where Comanche and bison ruled. The history of the Old West permeates the settlements, where many dreams died, and some still live on.

From the top of Capulin Volcano, where you can view five states, to the dramatic cut of the Canadian River in the depths of Mills Canyon, you feel spacious openness. Silence. Desolate beauty abounds. It is the kind of place a hermit might seek in her or his quest to catch a glimpse of the divine.

An old Spanish cemetery, called a *camposanto*, near Farley.

Sanctuaries

55. Dwan Light Sanctuary

Armand Hammer United World College of the American West
P.O. Box 248
Montezuma, NM 87731
505-454-4200

This little sanctuary is situated on the side of a ponderosa pine-studded hill, above the sacred Montezuma Hot Springs, and in the shadow of holy Hermit Peak. This location alone would render it extraordinary, but as you see when you come upon this unique place, this is only the beginning.

Upon first glance, the circular, stone exterior gives off a kiva-feeling. As you reach the large, wooden doors, you notice the windows, with gargantuan prisms situated inside of them, and you begin to wonder what's going on inside. No, this is not a dark, womblike kiva. Step through the small entry area into a round, stark, creamy-ivory chamber filled with colored rainbows and white-light reflections. It feels like magic. Like home to fairies. There is nothing else here besides a few candles and built-in *bancos* (benches) along the circular edges. Just you

Location: About 4 miles west of Las Vegas, N.M.

Description: A prism-designed sanctuary for people of all beliefs, named for its conceptual founder, Virginia Dwan.

Spiritual Significance: Magical light and silence.

Solitude Rating: ★★★

How to get there: Take I-25 to Exit 343, Grand Ave. Take this to New Mexico Ave. and turn left. Turn left again at Mills Ave. Go to Hot Springs Rd. and head west toward the mountains. It's 5 miles to campus and guest camping areas. (Or, take I-25 to Exit 343, Grand Ave., then follow the signs to the Historic Old Town Plaza.) Register at the campus administration building. You can drive or walk up the chapel, a short way up a small hill. Reservations appreciated.

Accessibility from highway: Easy.

Facilities: In Las Vegas, N.M.

Fee Area: No.

and the ever-changing color and shapes produced by the elegant design and placement of 12 large prisms in the sides and ceiling. The building and prisms are aligned to the cosmic light sources, catching beams from the sun, moon, and stars, and casting them in flowing ribbons of movement across the ceiling, floors, walls, and the fine hairs upon your skin. To sit in meditation here is to sit in the center of a kaleidoscope of change and color, much like our lives...awash in shifting reflections and angles on which to reflect.

Meditation pillows are available in a room to the side. Community meditation takes place several times a week (call 505-454-4211 for details). Before or after your quiet moments in the sanctuary, you may want to soak in the small hot-spring pools below, which are accessible from the highway. These pools are sacred waters, visited for centuries by native peoples; they are the primary reason this old resort, now the Armand Hammer United World College, exists.

These healing waters on the Gallinas River attracted the Santa Fe Railroad to build a resort in 1885. The first resort closed in 1903 when the railroad built another destination resort on the rim of the Grand Canyon. For 35 years thereafter, Montezuma's Castle was used as a seminary for Mexican priests. The Dwan Light Sanctuary was started in 1994 and dedicated in 1996. According to legend, Montezuma himself, the last great Aztec war chief, soaked in these waters.

Retreats

56. Mandala Center

Box 158
Des Moines, NM 88418
505-278-3002
www.mandalacenter.org

$\mathcal{M}$rs. Tish Hewitt, the daughter of the owner of John Deere Co., was being treated for manic depression in a Minneapolis hospital when she had a vision of two mountains that a spirit voice told her were in New Mexico. When she later traveled across country and saw these lands and mountains, she knew immediately that this was the place in her vision—and that she was meant to be here. The center began as her private, two-room residence in 1990, and quickly developed into her personal mandala, a series of round spaces and rooms. Following Mrs. Hewitt's death in 1992, her daughter, Anna, purchased the Mandala Center. Anna continues to work on the evolving vision: to build a place of peace where small groups and families can come to clear their minds, find spiritual renewal, and if necessary, heal their bodies. While Mrs. Hewitt may have died, she is still very present. She moves furniture, turns on lights in the night, and produces other acts of friendly ghost-dom.

The Mandala Center sits at 7,000 feet on the slopes of Sierra Grande, the largest freestanding mountain in the area. With access to 8,000 acres of the mountain for walks and exploration—and a vast volcanic landscape that includes Capulin Volcano National Monument—the feeling is spacious and serene. Although the highway passes below the center, it is a good distance away.

The Mandala Center, rooted in the Christian faith, is open to people of all faiths. With the purpose to "renew and refresh relationship with God,"

Location: East of Raton, 3.5 miles west of Des Moines, N.M.

Description: An interdenominational family and group retreat center with emphasis on leadership development for youth, spiritual development, health, and wholeness. Structured and unstructured retreat at 7,000 feet.

Solitude Rating: ★★★★

How to get there: On US 64/87, 3.5 miles west of Des Moines, N.M., at milepost 383 on the south side of the road.

Accessibility from highway: Fair.

Facilities: Food, lodging, and retreat for a set price, depending on the chosen event.

their programs are impressive. They offer a leadership program for youth in the summer; retreats in training, support, and personal spiritual development for patients with chronic and progressive diseases; and retreats for health-care practitioners in mind-body-spirit health care. The schedule includes offerings such as Heart Reconciliation & Right Relationships and intensive journal workshops. If your group is looking for a place to hold a retreat, program, or class, call the center to work out the logistics. The week I visited, the nearby women's club held a luncheon and then painted Mt. Capulin. Mandala also encourages solitary retreatants to come and walk, sleep, enjoy the sunset, observe nature, paint, and pray. Every day begins with an optional morning prayer group at 7:30 a.m.

Built with many local materials and imported woods, the modern and very beautiful lodge features comfortable sitting rooms, meeting rooms, a high-ceiling prayer room/chapel, a large kitchen, and a deck that overlooks the valley. The sleeping accommodations are very nice, though modest. Mandala accommodates different dietary needs, and guests say the food is delicious—even sinful—and wholesome at the same time.

Other Retreats

Casa del Gavilan B&B, Cimarron, 505-376-2246

Star Hill Inn, Sapello, 505-425-5605

Sacred Places

57. Capulin Volcano National Monument

P.O. Box 40
Capulin, NM 88414
505-278-2201
www.nps.gov/cavo/

*C*apulin Volcano erupted 62,000 years ago with "rooster tails" of spark and cinder and lava that covered almost 16 square miles. Today, this monument gives you the opportunity to travel to the top of the volcano, where you can take a short walk into its insides and view its vent. After a breather, you can walk up and around Mt. Capulin's rim to view the incredible high plains, full of other volcanic hills and mountains. It's all within easy reach. The drive to the top is a 2-mile paved road, the walk into the vent is 0.2 mile, and the trail around the crater rim is 1 mile.

In Spanish, *capulin* means "wild cherry." The name is reflected in the chokecherry trees that fill the volcanic cone, which is also the summer home for swarms of ladybugs. From its rim you see five states and many, many nearby volcanic hills and peaks. Sit with this mountain and hear its stories. You can almost see the pterodactyls flying through the smoke, ages ago, as Capulin exploded with fire and ash, sending streams of lava that glowed in the dark, from vents at her western base.

The best time for wildflowers at Capulin is late June and July, and a third of all visitors to Capulin come in July. Your best chance of finding quiet time on the mountain is to come any other month. (As solitude-seekers know, weekdays, early mornings, and late afternoons are best—it's in our blood!) The visitor center offers a short film on the volcano. At the base of the volcano, there is a picnic area and a 1-mile-long lava-flow trail.

The biggest disappointment of this special place is the traffic and the hours. For those seeking a more primitive approach, there is no trail for walking from the base to the top. And hours are short, with the volcano closing way before sunset (6:30 p.m.) in the summer, except on Friday and Saturday nights during June, July, and August. If you want some solitary time, this place presents a challenge—but be creative, because it's worth it.

Location: 33 miles east of Raton.

Description: This national monument is home to Mt. Capulin, a 1,300 foot extinct volcano on the high plains of northeastern New Mexico. Walk inside and witness the source of the earth's explosion. The total altitude is 8,182 feet above sea level.

Spiritual Significance: Volcano.

Solitude Rating: ★

How to get there: Head east from Raton on US 64/87, or go 58 miles west from Clayton via the same highway. A well-marked road heads north out of Capulin.

Accessibility from highway: Easy.

Facilities: Visitor center with a picnic area and bathrooms. No gas beyond Capulin.

Fee Area: Yes.

58. Hermit Peak

Las Vegas

This peak, once called El Cerro del Tecolote (Owl Mountain), is now named for a simple man from Italy, Giovanni Maria Agostini—a hermit. In the summer of 1863, Agostini traveled along the Old Santa Fe Trail from Council Grove, Kansas, to New Mexico. Legendary details of this trip hint that this was no ordinary old man; for example, offered a seat in one of the wagons on the long, strenuous journey, he refused.

Agostini was a character. Simple and poor, he carried letters of introduction from the likes of emperors and other influential people he met on his travels throughout the world. His journey began in Spain, France, and Italy. In 1838, he sailed to South America. In 1859, he lived in a cave in central

Mexico. From there, he journeyed to Cuba and Canada, and then gradually wandered to Kansas, where he encountered the Santa Fe Trail that brought him to the peak that would bear his name.

As is the pattern of his life, he came here to seek solitude. But as is also the pattern of his life, he aroused curiosity, and tales of his life abound. Agostini came to be known as a man with special spiritual powers who could heal the sick and offer prayers to the distraught. He made his home in a

Location: Just west of Las Vegas, N.M.

Description: Prominent, flat-topped mountain where spiritual ascetic Giovanni Maria Agostini, "the penitent hermit," lived in a cliff-side cave.

Spiritual Significance: Hermit-home, cave, spring, mountain.

Solitude Rating: ★★★★

How to get there: Take NM 65 west from Las Vegas, N.M. The paved road turns narrow and windy once you pass the Armand Hammer United World College. Go right when the road splits at about 14.5 miles, and continue to El Porvenir Campground. Park in the campground parking lot at about 17 miles. To climb the peak, walk to the self-service pay station in the campground and look for the Trail 223 sign to Hermit Peak. The trail is steep and strenuous, about 8 miles round-trip.

Accessibility from highway: Difficult.

Facilities: Water at the trailhead and at the spring on top of the mountain. Camping and toilets in the campground. Gas, food, and lodging in Las Vegas, N.M.

Fee Area: No.

shallow cave on the side of Hermit Peak, where he carved religious trinkets and crosses that he sold for barely enough money to buy the corn meal on which he survived. His neighbors, who called him Juan, placed him close to sainthood. He never asked for anything in return for the many blessings he bestowed. No doubt, he was surprised one day to see his neighbors make the precipitous trek to his mountainside home to build him a cabin. Agostini, in his mid-60s at the time, consented to their favor with the condition that the cabin have no windows and a door so small that he had to crawl through it on his hands and knees. In the midst of raising his log home, the great story goes, the builders ran out of water, atop the dry, scorched peak. Not willing to watch his friends suffer, Agostini scratched the ground with his walking stick and cool, miraculous spring water surged from the ground.

In 1867, Agostini left his mountain home and headed south. No one knows why, for sure. Perhaps his holy reputation catapulted him into a busier life than he liked. Perhaps, like so many of us beset by earthly possessions, his house became more than his simple, spiritual needs could bear. Two years after his departure, his body was discovered—with a dagger in his back—in a cave in the Organ Mountains, east of Las Cruces. His murderer was never found (see La Cueva, page 225).

People continue to make pilgrimages to this mountaintop. As they do at the sacred well down the road at Chimayo, they come to collect the sacred water that flows from the hermit's spring. Some make the trek barefoot, some wear fancy water bottles on hipside holders, and others carry plastic milk jugs. If you walk up the mountain, a side trail takes you to the hermit's south-facing cave, a few hundred feet below the top of the mountain cliff. Agostini's spring is the only source of water on the arid, flat mountaintop. La Sociedad del Ermitaño, a group that formed after the hermit's murder, built the crosses you see, in order to keep his holy example alive. Looking down the steep escarpment to the plains below, you can almost see the lines of wagons making their way along the Santa Fe Trail, bringing settlers—and one saint—to New Mexico.

El Porvenir, which means "the future," is where you begin your pilgrimage. As you walk up Hermit's Peak, you cannot help but feel the sacredness of your trek. You are walking in the steps of a holy man. You are retracing the tracks of La Sociedad del Ermitaño's annual Lenten pilgrimage up the peak. Up the steep, tangled trail you go, to the place of solitude, where Agostini kept company with the oldest spirits of the mountains— bristlecone pine, rock, and *el divina luz,* "the divine light" from the magnificent sunrise that sanctified them together.

You have trekked from "the future" to the past and into the ever-holy present.

59. Mills Canyon

Kiowa National Grassland
714 Main St.
Clayton, NM 88415
505-374-9652

*F*rom the highway, you have to drive 10 miles to reach this valley and the campground. You need a high-clearance vehicle—preferably a four-wheel-drive—for the steep, rocky trip. But it's worth every bit of effort, even if you have to rent a vehicle. Mills Canyon, cut by the Canadian River, is marvelous. I felt as if I had been dropped into the canyon lands of Utah, except these walls echo the New Mexico Plains Indian past of the Apache and Comanche.

The canyon is named for Melvin Mills, an attorney, territorial legislator, and businessman, a major player during the railroad days. In 1881, Mills built a two-story rock house and a bunkhouse for hired hands and began to establish a large orchard and cattle ranch. His orchard must have been a sight to see with more than 2,500 peach trees, 1,000 quince, 500 pear, 200 apple, as well as mulberry, cherry, apricot, nectarine, and plum. In his verdant canyon, Mills even grew nut trees—walnut, chestnut, pecan, and his own hybrid of soft-shelled almond. Not to mention acres of vegetables. Top this off with a stagecoach line coming down the cliffs to stop at the bottom of the canyon, and you are witness to another miracle of the past.

Alas, in 1904 the orchard met a torrential end when floods rampaged down the canyon, uprooting trees and burying the lands under 5 feet of silt.

Location: 10 miles northwest of Roy.

Description: Rugged, 900-foot deep canyon, habitat for mule deer, bear, Barbary sheep, Siberian ibex, and scads of birds and waterfowl.

Spiritual Significance: River, lush canyon, ancient Indian habitat, darkness, silence.

Solitude Rating: ★★★★

How to get there: From NM 39, turn west at Mills onto the marked road declaring the way to Mills Canyon. Note: Don't expect to see a town at Mills. It's on the map, but only a few remnants of a town remain.

Accessibility from highway: Remote and difficult.

Facilities: Few, including pit toilets and concrete picnic tables. Gas up in Roy or Springer. Once in the canyon, you're miles from conveniences and necessities.

Fee Area: No.

Mills attempted to rebuild, but finally abandoned his efforts in 1916. This powerful, pioneering Western attorney, who had escaped lynch mobs, lived through personal ridicule, and built a fortune, died in 1925, destitute.

As you enter the canyon, there is a marked campground to your right, which includes pit toilets and concrete tables. If you do not turn into the campground but continue on, you come to a fork in the road. The right fork takes you across the Canadian River and into lands of deeper privacy and beauty. The left fork, a short dead-end, passes the old homestead, heads into beautiful meadows, and ends with a stunning overlook of river and canyon walls.

I had the place to myself the weeknights I was here. Well, almost. Me and the incredible birds. I had never heard such a bird symphony at daybreak. Daylight brought a cacophony of color in the feathers of tanagers, buntings, warblers, and kingfishers, and that magical, changing light upon deep, ochre canyon walls.

Little is known about the lives that settled and passed through this canyon prior to Melvin Mills. A few tipi ring sites, with nearby chip stone material, have been found. Rock shelters high in the cliffs are thought to date back several thousand years. All else is mystery, here for you to absorb.

**Opposite: A vibrantly decorated chapel in
Montezuma is an eye-catcher under blue skies.**

Region Four

Southeast:
The Enchanted Lands

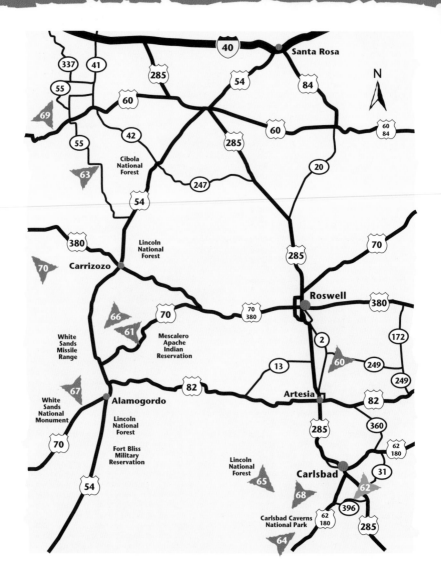

$\mathcal{W}$hile all of New Mexico is rightly called the "land of enchantment," there is no other part of the state that so imbues the feeling of mystery and magic than this one. It is, more than any other part of the state, the place of the unexpected. Images and surprises repeat themselves on a grand scale, filling the senses and keeping one in an almost continuous state of awe—from the boiling deserts of Carlsbad to the maple-covered Manzano Mountains that turn scarlet in the autumn, and from the Trinity Site of the first nuclear bomb explosion to the Three Rivers Petroglyphs and wondrous nearby Santo Niño de Atocha chapel. The difference here from the rest of the state isn't the magnitude of the events or spectacles—it's their proximity to one another upon the landscape, the way they coalesce to create a wide band of question and awe.

To visit here is to let yourself go, to be swept away by images and paradoxes that pervade and haunt you for days to come.

Sanctuaries

60. Miraculous Tortilla Shrine .... page **174**
61. Santo Niño de Atocha Chapel **176**
Other Sanctuaries **178**

Retreats

62. Black River Center for Learning **179**
Other Retreats **180**

Sacred Places

63. Gran Quivira Ruins **181**
64. Rattlesnake Springs **183**
65. Sitting Bull Falls **185**
66. Three Rivers Petroglyph Site **188**
67. White Sands National Monument,
    Alkali Flat Trail **190**

Spiritual Events

68. Mass Ascension, Carlsbad Bat Flights **192**
69. Mass Migration of Raptors,
    Manzano Hawk Watch **193**
70. Trinity Site **195**
Other Spiritual Events **198**

Sanctuaries
60. Miraculous Tortilla Shrine
203 Broadway
Lake Arthur, NM 88253

*L*ittle Maria Rubio, an older woman now, still gets goose bumps as she tells you about the morning Cristo appeared on a tortilla 23 years ago. It was a busy morning like every busy morning. Tortillas were a staple for Maria, her husband, Edward, and children (the couple eventually had five daughters and one son). According to Maria, at around 6:30 a.m. on

Location: On NM 2 between Roswell and Artesia.

Description: Home of Maria Rubio, to whom the face of Jesus appeared on a tortilla she was frying on October 5, 1977.

Spiritual Significance: Site of a miracle.

Solitude Rating: ★★★

How to get there: Take NM 2 to Lake Arthur and turn east on Broadway at the southern entrance to the town. Cross the railroad tracks and look for the second house on the left. Knock on the door before going around back to the shrine. Maria, who speaks very little English, graciously directs you to the shrine.

Accessibility from highway: Easy.

Facilities: In Roswell or Artesia. Lake Arthur has a small convenience store with gas.

Fee Area: No.

October 5, 1977, the brown, etched face of Jesus appeared on the surface of the tortilla she was heating. "I got goose bumps," she said as she rubbed her arm, "*Muy* happy." At the time, she was quoted in the *Chicago Tribune* as saying, "I do not know why this happened to me. But God has come into my life through this tortilla!"

Later, she thanked the tortilla for causing her husband to stop drinking and she claimed it helped her through a difficult pregnancy. As many as two dozen pilgrims a day—from all over the world—began to converge on her little house. Maria and her family built a tiny shrine in the backyard for the tortilla. Although the tortilla is dried and deformed at this point, a picture of it in better times verifies the clarity of the Cristo image.

Thousands have visited the small, crude shrine Maria built in her backyard, and the visitors agree that it is, indeed, a miracle. Just as much, it is vintage New Mexico, part of the wondrous Spanish/Mexican religious tapestry of the Lower Rio Grande that reaches into Texas to the Shrine of the Holy Camero, the Madonna Tree of Brownsville, and another tortilla shrine encased in plastic in Hidalgo. All of these shrines are considered places where God intervened and cured, a central theme of a devout and faithful spirituality and its marvelous, magical *mundo milagroso* (miraculous world).

61. Santo Niño de Atocha Chapel

Road 579, Three Rivers
Tularosa, NM 88352

$\mathcal{P}$erhaps you noticed the wooden statue of Santo Niño de Atocha, a young-child version of Christ, in the adjoining room at El Santuario de Chimayo (see page 61). In 1860, a little girl found the statue when she heard a church bell ringing beneath the ground. She called to her father and he, too, heard the bell. When he began to dig, he found the statue of Santo

Location: Between Tularosa and Carrizozo, directly east of Three Rivers.

Description: This little Catholic chapel in the remote Three Rivers area is one of the most moving and thought-provoking chapels you will see anywhere.

Spiritual Significance: Unusual church devoted to El Santo Niño de Atocha (The Holy Child of Antioch), patron saint of those unjustly imprisoned, protector of invalids, and divine doctor of illness. Canyon arroyo Stations of the Cross.

Solitude Rating: ★★★★★

How to get there: Take US 70/54 to Three Rivers. Turn east on County Road 830. The chapel is 4 miles past the entrance to Three Rivers Petroglyphs. Follow the small, carved wood signs.

Accessibility from highway: Fair.

Facilities: None.

Fee Area: No.

Niño. Many of the sick became well when they knelt before this statue. But you do not have to visit the chapel to be healed. Santo Niño is well-known for leaving his chapel at night, traveling the countryside on nocturnal visits of mercy and granting the requests of the many prayers he hears. His shoes are always well-worn, so the devout bring him new shoes to wear.

Devotion to El Santo Niño de Atocha originated in Spain about the 13th century, when the Moors were in frequent battle with the Christians. The Moors invaded the town of Atocha, holding many Christians captive and preventing the villagers from visiting the prisoners and bringing them food and water. One day a child appeared, carrying a basket of food and a gourd of water. The Moors allowed the child to bring the prisoners food and water every day, and although the prisoners ate heartily, the basket and gourd remained full. The people concluded that the child, unknown to the Christians or the Moors, must have been the child Jesus, disguised as a pilgrim, come to rescue them.

Paintings of El Niño often show him in a cloak with the St. James shell—a scallop shell and symbol of holy pilgrimages. Usually depicted holding a basket of either blessed bread or flowers, he wears sandals or is barefoot as he roams the hills and valleys at night, bringing aid and comfort to the needy, thereby wearing out his shoes.

I could not have guessed the profound beauty and powerful silence I would encounter when I opened the door to this sweet, small building. The little inscription on the outside of the church reads, "Since 1911." A pretty building with a red tile roof, it is nondescript as New Mexico churches go—until you step inside.

The sanctuary is filled with splendor. With all sizes of colorful, countless religious *bultos*, statues, and paintings, sacred images literally fill the church. Behind the altar stands El Santo Niño amidst a plethora of baby shoes that allude to his nightly wanderings. Candles burn devotion into the air. I felt the very essence of peace in this profound space and an intense love, signaled through the obvious care and beauty bestowed upon this sanctuary by each and every member of the congregation. On the back wall is a prayer, beseeching God for hearty crops on behalf of the farmer. Clearly, Santo Niño takes care of this farming and ranching community.

This congregation not only takes the care and adornment of its church to deeper levels, but their version of the life of this saint is also unique. They place their Santo Niño de Atocha originally in Antioch, Greece, where, according to a typewritten piece in the church, his *image* was one of the first images of Christ created. The artist was the apostle St. Luke, who later brought the first image of Christ to Spain. Thus, a revolution in religion took place. No longer was God delivered only through the word. Now, contact with the divine could be made through the image of Christ. When Santo Niño de Atocha comes to the prisoners to deliver the "bread and blood" of Christ, he provides Holy Communion and commences a spiritual feeding. The sheet also explains that El Niño carried butter in his sacred shell.

As you drive away from the church, back to the main road, there is a turnoff for the Stations of the Cross. A short drive up a gravel hill takes you to a dirt parking area and the entrance to an arroyo canyon. These 14 stations are truly magnificent, set amidst steep hills and water-shaven arroyo rocks. Erected in 1970, the stone monuments and metalwork images are as intrinsic and artful as the nearby century plants and ocotillos. Above the stations and the church, high upon Los Cerros de Don Pedro, stands La Cruz de Santo Niño, a tall mountaintop cross dedicated to El Niño. Dedicated to "the greater glory, honor and love to God," it was erected in 1964.

This place, juxtaposed against the mysterious petroglyph-studded hills a few miles away, holds more wonder than many better-known places.

Other Sanctuaries

St. Joseph's Apache Mission, Apache Cathedral, Mescalero

Retreats

62. Black River Center for Learning

1159 Black River Village Road
Carlsbad, NM 88220
505-785-2361
blackriver@carlsbadnm.com

The Black River environs have always been a location for change. From early Comanche and Apache inhabitants to retreatants today, humans have left their marks here over time. Look closely and you will see the mortar-and-pestle holes the Indians used to grind grains, seeds, and herbs. The lodge here was originally built in the 1920s. When traffic to Carlsbad Caverns became robust, the town of Black River took shape in the 1930s with a post office, gas station, grocery store, and restaurant. Alas, these businesses died when the highway to White City was finished. After several incarnations, this facility incorporated into the Black River Center for Learning (a ministry of the Tres Rios Area Christian Church) in 2000. It's available to all nonprofit groups. Elderhostel (a popular educational adventure group for the 55-and-over crowd), professional conferences, and family get-togethers all find Black River a hospitable, beautiful place.

Beyond the standard conference-center style, you'll discover a wonderfully equipped cafeteria, well-kept swimming pools, expansive playing fields, and dormitories. If you seek solitude, though, consider camping; if you'd prefer a solitary, indoor place at Black River, inquire about the new hermitages.

Location: South of Carlsbad on the confluence of the Black River and Castle Springs Creek.

Description: Retreat and conference center on 377 acres of desert beauty at 3,200 feet. Bring your own program and/or group for unstructured retreat.

Solitude Rating: ★★★

How to get there: Head south of Carlsbad on US 62/180, then turn east onto NM 396. All that remains of the town of Black River is the retreat center, formerly known as Tres Rios, which you will see on your right.

Accessibility from highway: Easy.

Facilities: All inclusive, gas in Carlsbad.

The most special thing is the setting. You can hike to old ranch ruins and Indian mescal pits across the river. The glorious Black River, once called Rio Azul Sacramento ("blue sacrament river"), lazily flows toward the Pecos here. Canoes and a paddleboat are available; a 2-mile (one-way) canoe trip takes you between beautiful canyon walls and into the territories of hummingbirds, cormorants, hawks, and countless songbirds. Birders can spy more than 30 species in a morning. Nearby lands host fox, cougar, bobcat, badger, javelina, turkey, coyote, and deer.

The warm and hospitable Black River Center offers days of peace and quiet as it maps out its destiny with change. The owners hope build various healing habitats, hermitages, a nature trail, a prayer trail, and a labyrinth. Special planned events include a Carlsbad Bat Breakfast weekend, Mescal Roast and Dances at the Living Desert Museum, and a Christmas on the Pecos boat ride. With Carlsbad Caverns and Rattlesnake Springs as neighbors, the Black River Center is in good, holy company.

Other Retreats

Casa Blanca B&B, San Antonio, 505-835-3027

Casa de Walela (Mountain Retreat Home of the Hummingbird), Tajique, 888-897-0027

Sufi Foundation of America, Torreon, 505-384-5135

Sacred Places

63. Gran Quivira Ruins

Salinas Pueblo Missions National Monument
P.O. Box 517
Mountainair, NM 87036
505-847-2587
www.nps.gov/sapu

*G*ran Quivira is one of three ruins that make up the Salinas Pueblo Missions National Monument (*salinas* is Spanish for "salt sources"). The other two ruins are Abo and Quarai.

As with many sites throughout New Mexico, the journey is as spiritual as the destination. If you come from the south, your ribbon of highway crosses beautiful, barren landscape and deserted towns with names such as Claunch. The theme of beauty and desolation continues as you enter the ruins, situated on a high plateau that offers views of the plains below. Solitude reigns as you begin your walk into the old village of the Rayodos (the "striped ones"), people who painted and tattooed broad lines over and under their eyes.

The people who lived here were hunters, farmers, and traders, an unusual mix that positioned their settlement to become one of the primary trade

Location: 25 miles north of Mountainair on NM 55.

Description: This Native American village, once known as Tompiro, is now called Pueblo de Las Humanas (thriving pueblo). A once-flourishing trade center, it was the object of Coronado's fruitless search for gold. Today, it hosts the remains of several kivas, along with churches that are a 150 years older than the oldest missions in California, Texas, and Arizona.

Spiritual Significance: Ruins, kivas, churches.

Solitude Rating: ★★★★

How to get there: Gran Quivira Ruins are off NM 55, north of Mountainair and north of Carrizozo. The turnoff is well-marked.

Accessibility from highway: Easy.

Facilities: Small visitor center with bathrooms and water.

Fee Area: No.

centers in this part of the world. Here, plains peoples came from the east, Rio Grande pueblo people from the west. Salt, rare and valuable, was the primary focus of trade. A survival staple for human and animal alike, salt was mined 24 miles north of here. The people also gathered pine nuts—which are 14 percent protein—from the surrounding piñon trees, then traded them. Corn and cotton were traded as well, in return for bison meat, hides, and other products from the eastern plains. It must have been a busy, bustling scene at times, anchored within a spiritual life and rituals to sustain the sacred corn: prayers to sow the seed, prayers to encourage growth, prayers for rain.

No doubt, rituals were carried out in the many kivas evident here. Every clan had their own kiva where sacred ceremonies took place in addition to other group work activities. The kivas were probably also used as lodging for guests. One large kiva at the Pueblo de Las Humanas may have been used for community-wide purposes. The surrounding saline basins, springs, and mountains marked the five sacred directions and the pueblo boundaries of the Salinas Pueblos.

Then there are the churches, the first finished in 1636. Construction on the second started in about 1660, around the time the friars burned and filled the sacred kivas in efforts to obliterate the religion. Not to be denied, the people moved their religious practices into ordinary pueblo rooms. The pueblo was abandoned in the 1670s, probably due to famine, Apache raids, and drought.

Kivas, churches, and endless tales of glory and pain...all are here today, powerful holy ghosts amidst high-desert breezes and the echo of a thousand voices.

64. Rattlesnake Springs

Carlsbad Caverns National Park
3225 National Parks Highway
Carlsbad, NM 88220
505-785-2232
www.nps.gov/cave/ratsprings.htm

Location: About 30 miles south of the entrance to Carlsbad Caverns National Park.

Description: A 13.5-acre desert oasis and wetlands fed by a large spring. A Nature Conservancy Preserve and detached unit of Carlsbad Caverns National Park.

Spiritual Significance: Spring, wetlands, rare birds, endangered reptiles and amphibians, prehistoric Indian and Mescalero Apache site.

Solitude Rating: ★★★★

How to get there: Take US 62/180 south of the Carlsbad Caverns National Park entrance; drive about 26 miles to County Road 418 until you see the sign for Rattlesnake Springs and Slaughter Canyon. Follow the signs to Rattlesnake Springs.

Accessibility from highway: Fair.

Facilities: A picnic area with tables and grills, drinking water, and toilets. No camping.

Fee Area: No.

*Y*ou feel the magnitude of this place as you enter. Instinctively, you know that in an earlier time, this oasis would have saved your life with its water and shade. The lushness would bring relief from the skin-shrinking desert that rendered you helpless in the piercing heat. It is a gathering site, where you would have congregated with others, perhaps lived, and certainly hunted. To walk this cottonwood forest today, amid the wetlands, springs, and towering trees, is to walk in the memory of a million dramas—from Indian to soldier to settler through the passage of time, with animals and full moonlight. Projectile points from Eddy County date back to 25,000 B.C.

Water sources are sacred because they are the origins and sustainers of life—especially in the harsh Chihuahuan Desert. Today, Rattlesnake Springs is the water source for Carlsbad Caverns National Park, as well as home to rare birds such as Bell's vireo, varied buntings, and green herons. Beside the running waters, you are a guest of butterflies, endangered eastern barking frogs, and western ribbon snakes.

This holy place. Come. Breathe the life force of oasis. See wild turkeys dart among the rabbitbrush. Glimpse a spray of vermilion from the flycatcher's wing. Follow a raucous kingfisher over the footsteps of an older time, into the ever-present sacred moment.

65. Sitting Bull Falls

Lincoln National Forest
Guadalupe Ranger District
Federal Building, Room 159
Carlsbad, NM 88220
505-885-4181
www.fs.fed.us/recreation/forest_descr/nm_r3_lincoln.html

The first thing people usually wonder about Sitting Bull Falls is the origin of its name. Did Sitting Bull, Lakota Chief and holy man, ever come here? According to one story, on a moonlit night in 1881, nine years before his death, Old Chief Sitting Bull led a party of braves that had stolen cattle and horses from ranchers in Seven Rivers (now White City, near the entrance to Carlsbad Caverns). A group pursued the Indians, and some say they witnessed the Indians eating a few of the horses. In their efforts to recover their property, however, the ranchers got lost and ended up at the falls. Thus, people named the falls for Sitting Bull. Others claim that Sitting Bull was never around the area and all the stories are just, well, a lot of bull.

What is true and clear about this place is the power and beauty of this spectacular oasis in the middle of the harsh, hot desert. Don't let the extensive and overdeveloped picnic site, parking area, and lower trail (complete with railings) put you off: (it's all so unlike the "simple"

Location: 52 miles southwest of Carlsbad.

Description: A emerald desert oasis with 150-foot waterfalls.

Spiritual Significance: Spring, waterfalls.

Solitude Rating: ★★★★

How to get there: Take US 285 north of Carlsbad to NM 137, then drive south and west. Follow NM 137 to FR 276 (County Road 409), which takes you into the falls.

Accessibility from highway: Fair.

Facilities: Picnic area, bathrooms, and water. Nice camping spots outside the picnic area in the National Forest. Gas up in Carlsbad.

Fee Area: Yes.

New Mexico we know and love.) While incongruous with the isolation and starkness you experienced on the picturesque drive into the falls, you soon move beyond the clutter on a short, well-marked walk to the falls. From the maintenance of the trail, I can only guess the developers were planning for lots of visitors. I found, if you go on a weekday, late or early, you will most likely have the place to yourself.

Strip down to your bathing suit (you do have one on, don't you?) and wade into the pools. They are heavenly. The water and the strongly proven negative ions immediately go to work on your sweat-drenched body as you soften and take in the scene: water-smoothed mountain cliffs; bright splashes of yellow, crimson, and purple flowers; hummingbirds that stroke the air; huge, dazzling dragonflies; and water cascading from high above you. It doesn't take long for bliss to saturate your desert-drenched soul.

On your way back to the parking lot, you'll see a sign for a trail to the top of the cliff. Put on a pair of sturdy hiking shoes and head up. Here you can move beyond concrete development and fencing. The uphill walk is short, strenuous, well-marked, and beautiful. At the top you're rewarded with more pools, trails, and to-die-for views. The trail continues into the canyon, a sublime walk into solitude.

66. Three Rivers Petroglyph Site

BLM Caballo Resource Area
1800 Marquess St.
Las Cruces, NM 88005
505-525-4300

There is something eerily special about this place. Perhaps it's the remoteness of the site and the miles of nothingness that surround you. Perhaps it's the mystery of the Jornada peoples who pecked the strange and wonderful images here or the unusualness of the images themselves. All combine to make this spot a place of wonder.

The Jornada Mogollon peoples were a group of prehistoric Indians who lived in this area around 1,000 years ago. Archeologists believe the petroglyphs in this area were made by Jornadas who inhabited a nearby village on the banks of Three Rivers creek for about 400 years. (An easy pathway connects the east side of the campground, crosses the road, and ends at the village.) By A.D. 1400, these peoples had abandoned their village for reasons unknown. Nobody knows where they went or who

Location: Approximately 35 miles north of Alamogordo, off US 54.

Description: More than 21,000 awesome petroglyphs created approximately 1,000 years ago, packed onto a small, rocky hill and basalt ridge with incredible views of the valley and mountains. Be sure and pick up the trail guide for the 0.5 mile trail with many offshoots.

Spiritual Significance: Petroglyphs, sacred Indian location, Indian ruins.

Solitude Rating: ★★★★

How to get there: Turn east from US 54 at Three Rivers onto County Road 830; travel 5 miles on paved road.

Accessibility from highway: Easy.

Facilities: Picnic area, water, and restrooms at the site. Campground down the road. No gas.

Fee Area: Yes.

their descendants would be today, leaving us to ponder the incredible images before our eyes, many that seem to speak of Mexico.

Among the images, you'll see animal bodies filled with geometric designs, bighorn sheep pierced by arrows, lion and bear tracks, and mysterious masks with almond-shaped eyes. Reptiles, clouds, plants, supernatural and otherworldly beings, human bodies inside fish, and circles of dots are here, too. The figures are prolific, one after another, scattered on and off the trail, which begins at the visitor shelter and ends at a terrific covered picnic area on the ridge. (If you're inclined to keep going, there are some glyphs beyond this point too.)

Why these drawings on this ridge? Most certainly it was a sacred site and perhaps a territorial boundary. The high vantage point also makes one wonder if it was a lookout point. It very likely could have been a stop on a trade route for those going north to earlier versions of Gran Quivira (see page 181). Seeking salt, perhaps? As you meander the ridge on numerous side trails, these inexplicable and powerful images conjure up a medley of explanations, from the wild to the sober. It's almost as if the Jornada peoples knew the future—as if they were attempting to anchor their spiritual world for a day in the future known as July 16, 1945. That was the day the first atomic bomb would be detonated 30 miles away at a place called Trinity, in the desert known as the Jornada del Muerto (Journey of the Dead Man).

67. White Sands National Monument, Alkali Flat Trail

P.O. Box 1086
Holloman AFB, NM 88330
505-479-6124
www.nps.gov/whsa/

*E*ntering White Sands is a perplexing exercise. The farther I drove into this landscape, the more my brain and body struggled to render the visual contradictions into a sensible response. Drifts of white surrounded me, and snow-moving equipment, including graders and front-loaders built to handle the worst of blizzards, lined the roads. The little buildings *must* be warming huts. My brain said snow, snow, until I stepped from my air-conditioned car into the piercing heat and the immensity of a million great dunes.

In the summer, the best time to visit White Sands is very early in the season or late in the day. If you go early in the day, plan to be off the dunes by 11 a.m. Or, better yet, go in the autumn, winter, or spring. When you go, wear a hat, sunscreen, and eye protection, and take plenty of water. Upon arrival, register at the trailhead. Follow the orange posts and spot your next marker in the distance before you continue to walk. There is no shade or formal resting area along this trail.

Location: 15 miles southwest of Alamogordo on US 70.

Description: 275 square miles of brilliant white gypsum dunes.

Spiritual Significance: Desert, ancient hunting grounds.

Solitude Rating: ★★★★★

How to get there: Go south on US 70 from Alamogordo for 15 miles to the park entrance. The trailhead is 7 miles from the visitor center, at the end of the road.

Accessibility from highway: Easy.

Facilities: Gas and lodging in Alamogordo. A visitor center at the park with bathrooms and water. Picnic areas out in the dunes.

Fee Area: Yes.

There is nothing, nothing else like these White Sands. The white gypsum shimmers and sparkles. And when you begin to walk upon them, you realize you can do so easily and still stay on top (unlike the Great Sand Dunes in Colorado, where you sink in and walking is a chore). These sandy hills, akin to packed sugar, are cool to the feet.

The trail for spirit-seekers is the Alkali Flat Trail, a 4.6-mile loop across alabaster dunes that stretch into forever. Upon this trail, out of sight from all that is manmade, you feel the expanse and calmness of the universe. Rolling white set against the jutting San Andres Mountains. Slowly you move, through the Heart of the Sands, across ridges of white, down dune sides and up again. On and on, over and over, until you come to the vast, flat expanse of the dry bed of Lake Otero. Here, 10,000 years ago, Pleistocene hunters speared giant bison. Here, 7,000 years ago, grasslands began to give way to desert. As recently as 1,000 years ago, two large pueblos thrived beside Lake Lucero, a short distance to the south. Eventually, the Tularosa Basin, where you stand, became a for bidding alkali desert, a harsh terrain that the more-recent Mescalero Apache viewed from their surrounding mountain homes.

If you walk this journey alone, I doubt you will return from this loop without some sense of ecstasy or a feeling that your spirit has been fed in a very extraordinary way. If nothing else, consider your body moving through dunes born of howling winds and extreme temperatures. Dunes in ever-constant movement, a product of lakes that beget the crystalline grains and of mountains that force the winds to release their gritty bounty. Besides water, a journal may be in order.

Spiritual Events

68. Mass Ascension, Carlsbad Bat Flights

April/May–October/November
Carlsbad Caverns National Park

Photo by Wendy Shattil

*Y*ou're never quite sure what they're going to do. At sunset, the bats may dribble up and out from the mouth of their cave, over a long period of time, until it gets too dark to see them. Or, the half-million or so winged mammals may gush from the ground in a 20-minute spectacle sure to set your soul a-spin. In rainy weather, you're pretty much assured of the latter, since the bats stayed inside for a night. Regardless of the whims of their nighttime emergence, you are witness to their spiral into the skies, perhaps accompanied by a silhouetted deer upon the surrounding mesa and the flurry of 2,000 cave swallows.

Or, you can come at dawn, when you may have the place to yourself, and when magic envelops the scene. At daybreak, when light seeps into night, the bats make their way from faraway fields to their summer breeding cave, a quarter mile into the ground. The scene is amazing: skies of lavender tangerine, canyon wrens filling the morning with trill, big-racked bucks meandering above you, as a dark trail of bats takes form for as far as you can see. They come from the east, the rising sun pushing them toward you. Thousands upon thousands of zipping bodies. The lighter it gets, the more bats you see. Unlike the evening, when they spiral out in counterclockwise motion, their return is a stunning dive from hundreds of feet above, at 25 mph or more. A wild and wonderful chaos of wing, amidst prehistoric calls that place you in otherworldly time.

Mexican freetailed bats are truly amazing creatures. Contrary to popular belief, bats aren't blind. But as darkness falls, they rely more on their keen sonar than on sight. The bats can fly as high as 10,000 feet and have been clocked at speeds of 65 mph. On a given night, looking for food, they travel 50 to 60 miles. And yet they are one of us—mammals that breast-feed their young. Around April or May, these migrating bats arrive at their Carlsbad home to give birth and to feed on the plentiful insect supply. They depart in October or November for Mexico. They've been coming here for 5,000 years.

I recommend that you go in the evening. (Call ahead to find out the projected time of their exit, which changes throughout the season.) Attend the ranger's fascinating preflight talk and see what will unfold in the evening. But be forewarned—the amphitheater holds 1,000 people, so you may have lots of company. Once you have the basics down from this visit, go back at dawn, as the desert awakens in silence and song, and the bats return to rest their velvety bodies.

Located at 3225 National Parks Highway, Carlsbad, NM, 88220, adjacent to the visitor center at Carlsbad Caverns. Call 505-785-2232 or check out www.nps.gov/cave.

69. Mass Migration of Raptors, Manzano Hawk Watch

September–November, Manzano Mountains State Park

Every autumn they gather, those who dearly love the great birds and the great outdoors. From a spectacular, 9,200-foot vantage point high in the Manzano Mountains, they sit and count as the big birds fly by, a few feet above. Hundreds upon hundreds of sharp-shinned hawks, Swainson's hawks on their way to Argentina, massive redtails gliding the thermals, kestrels (sparrow hawks) zipping, turkey vultures soaring, golden eagles filling the sky with a wing, and peregrine falcons perusing the mountaintop and plunging from the clouds. And you are invited to this party of wonderment!

Hawk Watch is an international organization that monitors the spring and autumn raptor migration. Through knowledge of population trends, the organization ascertains ecosystem health and promotes action to protect the birds. Along the way, they make some exciting discoveries, such as the recent confirmation that the gregarious broad-winged hawk is moving into the West.

The Manzano site is the only autumn Hawk Watch in New Mexico. On the day I arrived, I was greeted by two vibrant and warm, twenty-something

The Manzano Hawk Watch can be a spiritual experience; pictured here is a Swainson's hawk.

Photo by Wendy Shattil.

young folks, eating salmon out of cans and offering impromptu information. Don't worry if you're new to bird-watching. You can show up on the mountain and the devoted will take you under their wings, and teach you what you need to know.

The Hawk Watch is active from around Sept. 1 to Nov. 5. The prime times for big numbers of birds—as well as people—are the last week of September and the first week of October, when you might count 300 to 400 a day. The hours from 10:30 a.m. to 1 p.m. are primo. The hawk watchers also catch, band, and release, giving participants an incredible opportunity to see the birds, for a very short time, close up. And perhaps you will be chosen to release one of them back into the sky.

Holy events such as these stop you in your tracks. Migration is a wondrous, mysterious marvel. The birds' freedom and flight are glorious. In watching this phenomenon on this crucial flyway, you join the spirits of those who came before you, others who walked this mountain ridge and knew this spot as a very special place to view birds. Not far from where you sit is an ancient catch pit. The birds you watch are a central element of Pueblo spirituality—birds are their messengers to the Gods and their feathers are offered as prayers to the spirit realm. Feathers are attached to prayer sticks and then planted, and loose feathers are offered to an altar, placed under stones or cast into rivers or lakes.

Birds, many Native Americans believe, possess magical properties. Like our very own breath, they travel through the air, mediums for messages and prayer. After a short watch on this mountain in the autumn sun, you too, will feel their breath of spirit.

The Hawk Watch site is located on Capilla Peak. Go to the town of Manzano, on NM 337, southeast of Albuquerque. Take Forest Road 245 from Manzano to the top of the mountain and look for the Hawk Watch signs and the Gavilan Trailhead (in Spanish, *gavilan* means "sparrow-hawk"). Take this relatively easy 0.5-mile trail to the observation site, not far from the fire towers. High-clearance and/or four-wheel-drive vehicles are certainly a help, but not necessary. There are campgrounds on top. Call Hawkwatch at 800-726-4295, or visit their website, Hawkwatch@vii.com.

70. Trinity Site

First Saturday in April and October
White Sands Missile Range

An eerie sensation envelops this desolate spot. You come because something devastatingly omnipotent and life-changing happened here. And, perhaps, you come to add your prayers that the earth might be healed and humankind might know hope. But the 2,400-foot diameter crater, once as much as 10 feet deep, has been filled and pieces of concrete foundations are all that remain of the observation towers. There's really not much to see. Yet, when people approach this site, they do so in awed silence and reverence. They speak in quiet, low voices and shed tears to the desert ground below their feet.

A simple, black, lava-rock monument protrudes from the flat, barren lands of this valley called Jornada del Muerto (Journey of Death). These lonely lands were once taken as a "shortcut" on the Camino Real, digressing from the Rio Grande, where it turned west and narrowed. Here, early travelers and wagon trains opted for a 60-mile desert detour. Here, for centuries before the atomic bomb was detonated, this dreary, scorching wasteland stole life away through starvation, thirst, debilitating fatigue, and Apache arrows.

Then, on July 16, 1945, at 5:29:45 MST, a nuclear bomb was triggered that would shake windows as far to the west as Silver City, and would prompt a blind person to see its flash from more than a 100 miles away. A flash brighter than a dozen suns, with a heat 10,000 times hotter than the surface of our own precious *sol*.

The government considered other locations—some spectacularly beautiful—for this explosion. It could have been in the San Luis Valley of Colorado, where I used to live; in the lava beds at El Malpais National Monument (see page 48); or in bird-rich and beautiful Padre Island off the Texas coast. When the government selected this site over another "finalist" in California, participant and 1938 Nobel Prize-winning physicist Enrico Fermi was willing to bet his cohorts that the test would wipe out all life on earth, with sure destruction of the state of New Mexico.

As with most spiritual sites in this book, various tales to sort and ponder abound. According to the most popular and repeated story, the code name "Trinity" came from J. Robert Oppenheimer, the leader of the scientists who converged on the area for this project in the spring of 1943. Oppenheimer supposedly drew the name from "Holy Sonnet 14" by 17th-century poet and clergyman John Donne.

> Batter my heart, three person'd God; for, you
> As yet but knock, breathe, shine, and seek to mend.

Another story, however, goes without challenge: Upon witnessing the awesome blast, Oppenheimer quoted a line from the *Bhagavad-Gita,* a sacred Hindu text: "I am become death, the shatterer of worlds."

The lava rock monument bears two plaques. The first reads "Trinity Site Where the World's First Nuclear Device Was Exploded on July 16, 1945." The second, added in 1975, reads, "This site possesses national significance in commemorating the history of the U.S.A." The National Park Service added it when they designated the Trinity Site a National Historic Landmark.

But perhaps the strongest, most powerful memorial of this lonesome place comes twice a year, when long lines of cars arrive, and people filter out, full of prayers. Some conduct religious services. Others pray for peace. Many just stand and stare and steady their breath. All, it can safely be stated, join the throngs of humanity for whom this event raised questions of power, philosophy, religion, and the very existence of all things that dwell on Earth.

Personally, I cannot separate this site from the place down the road called Three Rivers Petroglyphs (see page 188), where eerie and mysterious drawings on rocks seem almost to prophesy this event. Or the presence of Mary Magdalene (see Lady on the Mountain, page 227), across the valley,

The world's first atomic bomb test detonation occurred at the Trinity Site.

Photo by William Stone.

high upon the mountaintop, who shelters her throngs in peace. Trinity Monument lies almost on a straight line in between the two. Like a stake in the heart of spirit.

This site is open only twice a year—the first Saturday in both April and October, from 8 a.m. to 2 p.m.—and there is no fee to visit. It is located 60 miles northwest of Alamogordo, about 100 miles south of Albuquerque. To get there, take I-25 to the San Antonio turnoff, and proceed 12 miles on US 380 to the Stallion exit, NM 525/Range Road 7. Turn south, register at the gate 4 miles down the road, and proceed 17 miles to the ground-zero site. It is a 0.25-mile walk from the parking area to the ground-zero site and monument. I recommend going early to avoid delays with parking.

Besides porta-potties, there are no facilities, no water and no picnic tables. If you bring your own food you must eat in your vehicle. Or, stop in San Antonio at the Owl Café (505-835-9946). More than just a place to appease the palate, the café has the best green chile cheeseburger around, and a rich and whimsical atmosphere. And history. The men from the

Manhattan Project came down the road from the Trinity site and frequented this restaurant. It's open daily except Sunday.

For information on the Trinity Site and tours, call the Alamogordo Chamber of Commerce (800-826-0294) or check out their website at www.alamogordo.com.

Other Spiritual Events

Apache Maidens' Puberty Rites, July 4, Mescalero Apache, 505-761-4494

Luminaria Festival, Christmas Eve, Tularosa, 505-585-9858

This stone gate in Mountainair depicts a devilish visage.

Opposite: Tree shrine at Santo Niño de Atocha Chapel east of Three Rivers.

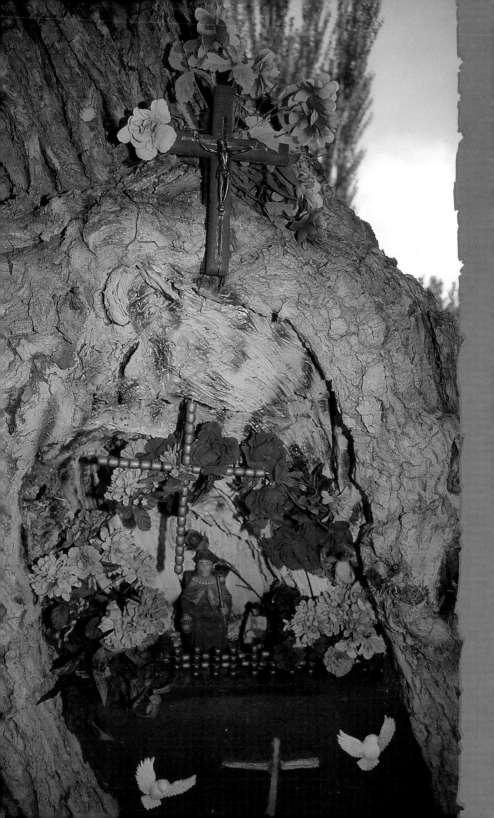

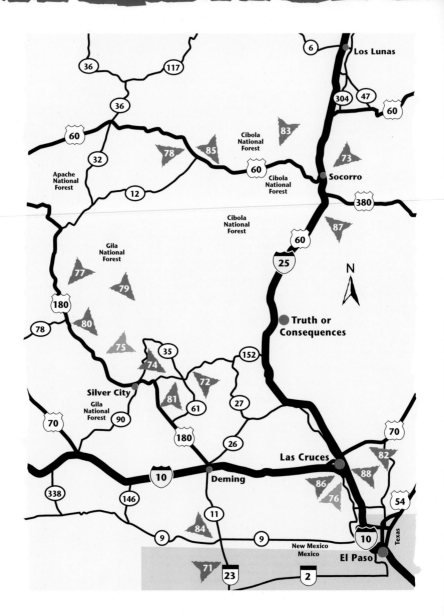

From stunning canyons and precarious catwalks over water, to the first federally-designated Wilderness Area, to the last foreign invasion of the United States, this section of New Mexico will appeal to the seeker and adventurer. Here, you find monstrous radio telescopes that constantly listen to outer space and piece together spectacular images of the dark unknown. They are just down the road from the image of Mary Magdalene on the mountainside in Magdalena. The imagination wanders as you cross the wide, barren, grassy Plains of San Agustin and the imagination cringes as you think about those who perished on the scorching desert of the Jornada del Muerto (Journey of Death).

In a strange way, it is fitting that the hermit who had inhabited the cave atop Hermit Peak near Las Vegas, N.M. (see page 166) came to a murderous end in another cave here, outside Las Cruces in the Organ Mountains. For New Mexico is nothing if not a fascinating collage of contradiction: first the home to Indian peoples who spread out upon her lands, and later home to a lonely Spanish outpost, isolated by deserts, hostile Indians, and mountains. This region encapsulates it all—the ruins of early peoples, the rich copper mine of Santa Rita, and El Camino Real, a lifeline route from deep within Mexico.

The hermit died here, as did the dreams of many adventurers and seekers. But the spirit lives on.

Sanctuaries

71. **Our Lady of Guadalupe Church** 202
72. **San Lorenzo Mission** 204
73. **San Miguel Church** 206
74. **Santa Rita Shrine** 208
Other Sanctuaries 209

Retreats

75. **Casitas de Gila** 210
76. **Holy Cross Retreat** 212
Other Retreats 213

Sacred Places

77. **The Catwalk** 214
78. **Datil Well Woodlands** 216
79. **Gila Cliff Dwellings** 218
80. **Gila Riparian Preserve** 221
81. **Kneeling Nun Mountain** 222
82. **La Cueva** 225
83. **Lady on the Mountain** 227
84. **Pancho Villa Memorial** 229
85. **Very Large Array (VLA)** 232

Spiritual Events

86. **Dia de los Muertos Celebration,**
    Calavera Coalition 234
87. **Mass Ascension, Water Birds** 236
88. **Pilgrimage in Honor of**
    La Virgen de Guadalupe 238

Sanctuaries

71. Our Lady of Guadalupe Church

On the Plaza
Palomas, Chihuahua, Mexico

$\mathcal{W}$hy include a place in Mexico in a book about New Mexico? Once you stand on Coote's Hill, looking south into Mexico from Columbus, the most natural inclination is to dip south. It's an easy, safe walk across the border into the flavor, charm, and poverty-driven discomfort of Old Mexico. Visiting this site completes the loop of understanding and the rewards are great. Even today, you get a hint of what Pancho Villa was fighting for (see Pancho Villa Memorial, page 229). This city, Palomas, was established in 1890, the same year as Columbus, New Mexico.

Our Lady of Guadalupe Church is a magnificent example of simple beauty. Off the bustling plaza, the church is the spiritual home to the people of Palomas. The name of the town, Palomas, means "pigeon" or "dove," suggesting the Holy Spirit. The church's doors are open, and it's common to see a destitute Mexican man in prayer, making his way around to the various images of Mary, kissing them in humble supplication.

Location: Palomas, Mexico, is 3 miles south of Columbus, New Mexico (see Pancho Villa Memorial, page 229).

Description: A strikingly beautiful stone church in the heart of the quaint Mexican village of Palomas, a town of 8,000 people that features bakeries, tortilla factories, a new cinema, and sidewalk vendors.

Spiritual Significance: Beautiful stone church dedicated to our Lady of Guadalupe.

Solitude Rating: ★★★★

How to get there: Drive south on NM 11 from Columbus, N.M., to the Mexico border. Park in the parking lot on the right side of the highway, just before you come to the border. You can walk across the border—you do not need a passport or tourist visa for a one-day visit. Continue down the street for two to three blocks and turn right onto the plaza. The church is on the west side of the plaza.

Accessibility from highway: Easy.

Facilities: I recommend the shopping, food, water, and restrooms at La Tienda Rosa (The Pink Store) on Main Street, within sight of the border. Their Pancho Villa Restaurant and Bar is fabulous and safe—even the ice is made with purified water—and you get a free margarita as you shop. Unlike most border-town stores, this is not a place where you bargain. The prices are already low and no one pressures you.

Fee Area: No.

The inside of the church is in disrepair, with cracks, leaks, and a raised, warped floor. An old, dusty foot organ stands along one side and stick-on colored paper on the windows provides a stained glass effect. And yet, there is something powerfully moving within these walls.

Behind the church is a large, concrete building featuring large stained-glass windows and theater-style benches to house the worshipping throngs. A life-size image of Our Lady of Guadalupe stands on the altar. The warehouselike building is so large that birds fly back and forth above you, inside.

These houses of worship stand side by side, an apt metaphor for old Old Mexico and new Old Mexico. She is a land that continues to struggle, where opportunity does not come to all peoples. It is worth the trip to remind us of our gifts and the beauty that exists in all eyes.

72. San Lorenzo Mission

San Lorenzo, NM 88041
505-536-9405

San Lorenzo, one of the prettiest little villages in New Mexico, was named by Lorenzo Lopez to commemorate not just his patron saint, St. Lawrence, but also his own name. This quirky story makes sense, for as soon as you enter this village you perceive a different pulse. There are the olden, historic adobes. And then there is the Sisters Restaurant, which many (including me) claim as a unique, spiritual experience. Sisters (not the nunnery kind) Nancy and Rita showed up late at a garage sale here in 1991. When they discovered all that was left to buy was the building, they snatched it up, and then proceeded to transform the old store and saloon into an exquisite dining "home." The sisters do the cooking themselves, including homemade breads, desserts, and a pastrami sandwich to die for. It is, simply, heavenly. As with all spiritual endeavors, patience is important. The food doesn't come fast, but the laughter, guffaws, and sudden exclamations from the kitchen keep you entertained. Call first for hours—these characters are proud to say they take a lot of days off (505-536-9888).

Just down the street from the Sisters Restaurant is the Mission of San Lorenzo, named for the Patron Saint of Libraries and Librarians, noted for forbearance and grace under pressure (he would have done well at Sisters). This adobe church, built in the 1880s, is a tribute to San Lorenzo and this

Location: About 20 miles east of Silver City.

Description: Beautiful, quaint mission built in the late 1800s in the picturesque village of San Lorenzo.

Spiritual Significance: A simple and lovely center of worship.

Solitude Rating: ★★★★

How to get there: Turn off NM 152 and follow the signs into the village. The mission is on the north end of town, off Galaz Street (the main street going through town). An obvious diagonal street, named San Lorenzo, leads you right to it.

Accessibility from highway: Easy.

Facilities: None.

Fee Area: No.

region's rich history. A beautiful, holy simplicity dwells here. Be sure to visit the shrine room, off to the left of the altar.

San Lorenzo, the archivist of the Christian church of the third century, was believed to have a list of all the members of the early church as well as the locations of gold supposedly hidden by the popes. Captured by the Romans in August, A.D. 258, he was given two days to deliver the names and treasures to the imperial palace. Lorenzo instead gathered up orphaned, sick, and crippled Christians, brought them to the palace and pronounced, "These are the treasures of the church!" The emperor was not amused. According to one version of the story, on the site of the Basilica di San Lorenzo in Rome, the emperor slowly roasted Lorenzo on a grill in an effort to force the information from his parched lips. Thus, in another odd twist of fate, San Lorenzo is also considered a Patron Saint of Cooks—a sure muse for the Sisters. One parable "pits" Lorenzo in defiance to the end, insisting to his executioners, "Turn me over—I am done on this side."

San Lorenzo's feast day, August 10, is celebrated here in San Lorenzo and at the Picuris Pueblo (see San Lorenzo Feast Day, page 153). The feast occurs not only on the anniversary of the Pueblo Revolt, but near the Perseid meteor showers, referred to as "The Tears of St. Lawrence" in Italy.

73. San Miguel Church

403 El Camino Real
Socorro, NM 87801
505-835-1620
smiguel@sdc.org

*W*hen explorer Juan Oñate's exhausted expedition trudged into this area in 1598, after crossing the barren, hot lands known today as the Jornada del Muerto (Journey of Death), the natives of Pueblo of Pilabo assisted them with food and water. From that momentous time, this area was known as El Pueblo de Nuestra Señora del Socorro (The City of Our Lady of Aid). In Spanish, *socorro* means "aid" or "help."

The first mission, Nuestra Señora de Socorro, was built in 1626 along this route known as El Camino Real. Today's splendid church was built in 1815, upon the ruins of the original building, which was destroyed in the Pueblo Revolt of 1680. The natives of Pueblo of Pilabo did not join the Pueblo Revolt. Instead, they fled south to Texas with the Spanish, never to return. Their ancestors still live in west Texas, in a place they call Socorro del Sur (Socorro of the South).

The church is named for San Miguel, a Roman Catholic saint also known as Saint Michael the Archangel. Considered a spiritual messenger (in Hebrew, the word angel means "one going" or "one sent"), San Miguel is the leader in the triumph of heaven over hell, in the battle fought at the end of time against Satan. (San Miguel actually takes on Satan twice—this is the second battle.) One of the most popular saints throughout New Mexico—like Guadalupe— you see San Miguel's name applied to churches, mountains, counties, and towns. No doubt, his popularity stems from the fact that he shares the experiences of war and strife with the people of New Mexico. San Miguel, leader of the heavenly armies, is often pictured in the final judgment with a set of scales, a symbol of his reputation for fairness, as he weighs the souls of the risen dead.

Location: In the heart of Socorro, 72 miles south of Albuquerque.

Description: A resplendent mission church originally built in 1626.

Spiritual Significance: An early church on El Camino Real.

Solitude Rating: ★★★★

How to get there: Socorro's plaza is just west of I-25. The church is off the north side of the plaza on El Camino Real.

Accessibility from highway: Easy.

Facilities: All amenities in the town of Socorro.

Fee Area: No.

The graceful San Miguel Mission immediately strikes you with its vast and awesome carved-wood ceiling and its strange and wonderful shape. But it's the colorful, larger-than-life figures on the altar that capture your imagination. They look as if they are acting out a fascinating drama—an apt metaphor for this place of heavenly armies and aid.

Long after the Pueblo Revolt, a second wave of settlers arrived here in 1815, established their homes, rebuilt the church, and set to work cultivating the verdant fields between the Rio Grande to the east and the mountains to the west. Legend has it that an Apache raiding party approached the unprotected settlement, but jettisoned their planned attack when they saw an angel hovering above the mission church. Thus, the people named their church after the Archangel, San Miguel. This tale is very similar to the story of Magdalena Mountain (see Lady on the Mountain, page 227). Perhaps it's not surprising that the parishioners of San Miguel make an annual pilgrimage from Magdalena to Socorro.

74. Santa Rita Shrine

Hanover, NM 88041

*W*ithin sight of the Kneeling Nun rock monolith (see page 222) and the colossal pit of the Santa Rita Mine, is the shrine to Santa Rita, a grassy, outdoor sanctuary of peace that sits above the traffic that travels and turns below. Santa Rita, born of parents of advanced age in Spoleto, Italy, in 1381, wanted to become a nun. Instead, she carried out the will of her parents and married at age 12. Although her husband was very cruel and mean, she remained a dutiful wife and mother for 18 years, until her husband was

Location: In Hanover, about 12 miles east of Silver City.

Description: A deeply touching, handmade shrine to Santa Rita, which includes a memorial to local Vietnam veterans.

Spiritual Significance: Neighborhood shrine.

Solitude Rating: ★★★

How to get there: The shrine is at the junction of NM 152 and 356, just east of Silver City, on the southwest hilltop corner. There is room at the intersection to pull over and walk up to the shrine, or you can drive around and come in from the back.

Accessibility from highway: Easy.

Facilities: Benches only.

Fee Area: No.

murdered. (Sometimes, God's ways are not so mysterious!) When her twin sons became intent on seeking revenge for his murder, Rita appealed to God to take her sons rather than have them commit murder. When they both died, she applied for admission to the Augustinian convent at Cascia. Due to her status as widow, she was refused. Through fasting, penance, good work—and some say, divine intervention—she was finally admitted. One day while in prayer, she asked to suffer like the Divine Savior. She was struck in the forehead by a thorn from Christ's crucifix, leaving stigmata, a deep wound that never healed. Saint Rita, Patroness of Impossible Cases, is known for many miracles.

This stone and concrete shrine to Saint Rita is sweet and quaint. You are struck by the painted pink benches that embrace this special place. Many plastic roses, her symbol, and votive candles hug her life-size image within the glass case.

In front of her peaceful image stands a square memorial to Vietnam veterans killed in action. Vases made of shell casings hold flags above the words, "All gave some—some gave all." A simple rose bush grows in front.

Other Sanctuaries

Our Lady of Guadalupe Shrine and Parish, Mesilla Park, 505-526-8171

San Albino Mission Church, On the Plaza, La Mesilla

Retreats

75. Casitas de Gila

310 Hooker Loop
P.O. Box 325
Gila, NM 88038
877-923-4827
www.casitasdegila.com

*W*hen I asked Becky and Michael O'Connor, the hosts and owners, what makes this place so special, they didn't hesitate. Becky said it's nature—birds, bobcats, bighorn sheep, mule deer, and the occasional mountain lion. Then, she added silence to her list, plus the fact that there's no light pollution. Nightfall unfolds an expansive, starlit sky. Michael nodded and agreed, and then added his own reason—these lands are old Indian lands, full of stories and shrines.

Just across the way, on top of Turtle Rock (see photo above), are two kivas that date back to the prehistoric Mimbres Indians, famous for their

Location: 4 miles northeast of Gila (pronounced HE-la).

Description: Unstructured retreat in five cozy, southwestern style guest houses located on a cliff overlooking Bear Creek, to the south of the Gila Wilderness.

Solitude Rating:
★★★★

How to get there: Call for reservations and directions.

Accessibility from highway: Fair.

Facilities: Completely furnished, comfortable guest houses. Bring your own food. Restaurants and gasoline in Gila.

beautifully painted and decorated pottery. Turtle Rock, within sight of all rooms, is a powerful focus for contemplation. A single route takes you to its massive top—a feature that prompted the Mimbres to use it for spiritual retreat, and later, for the Apache to secure her as a stronghold and hiding place.

Yes, this place is unique. As I drove in, a rainbow sprang from the sky and ended about 30 feet from the car. The five little guest houses perch exquisitely along the rim of the canyon, where Bear Creek flows serenely below. Named for the environs that embrace, the houses are *casitas del sol y la luna, flores, pajaros, animalitos,* and *arboles* (little house of the sun and moon, flowers, birds, small animals, and trees, respectively). Each house is designed and furnished around its theme. For special moments, a hot tub sits on the bluff under endless sky and within view of the ever-changing light show on the cliffs.

Casitas de Gila has no TVs, but there are phones in the rooms. If you choose to stay in your room, you will find comfort, a fireplace, and fascinating books on natural history and the Southwest. But chances are good you will take to the lands. A short walk down the bluff puts you next to the stream, where a hammock invites you to dawdle. Cross the stream, and you are privy to game trails, more than 600 acres of state lands, and even more national forests.

Nobody makes decisions for you here. You come, you stay, you cook what you please and when you please, all within the quiet confines of a beautiful place. If you're coming for retreat, tell Becky and she will give you a room away from any extra activity. This will help, but keep in mind that children are allowed, some guest houses adjoin, and all the houses are close to one another.

Michael, a geologist, welcomes a chance to show you the minerals of the area. If you want to travel via horseback, there's a ranch next door. It's all up to you, to create your space and let nature do her work to set your soul at ease.

76. Holy Cross Retreat

600 Holy Cross Road
P.O. Box 159
Mesilla Park, NM 88047
505-524-3688
www.zianet.com/franciscan

Since Las Cruces is in the heart of the Chihuahuan Desert, when you enter Holy Cross via a lush, tree-lined lane, bordered with Stations of the Cross, you immediately feel you are in a distinctively elegant place. Spacious grounds, architectural beauty, and attention to detail all contribute to a place of calm and serenity. This grand hacienda, originally built by Frank Monaghan in 1913, was known for many years as the Monaghan Ranch. In 1954, the Franciscan Order of Santa Barbara, California, purchased the home —complete with some stunningly beautiful furnishings such as the hand-carved, Japanese dining-room set—and 19 acres. The home embraces you, as you move from the large living room with its awesome fireplace and antique ebony piano to the quaint and cozy sun-filled atrium with tables, chairs, and fountain. This warm, inviting space opens onto the kivalike chapel with its wall of fascinating crosses and crucifixes of many sizes and styles.

Location: 3 miles south of Las Cruces.

Description: An ecumenical retreat and conference center, run by the Conventual Franciscan Friars, set in a beautiful pecan grove on spacious, rural grounds.

Solitude Rating: ★★

How to get there: From Las Cruces, drive south on Main Street (NM 478). Turn left onto Pecan Drive, just past the light for Carver Road. Follow Pecan Drive to the end and bear right into Holy Cross.

Accessibility from highway: Easy.

Facilities: All inclusive. Gas in the city.

The grounds of the retreat center include 46 motel-type rooms that can house up to 132 at a time, each with a private bath. The dining room serves buffet-style and can accommodate up to 150. The home-cooked traditional Mexican cuisine smelled yummy, but I didn't get to eat the day I was there.

Holy Cross offers both structured and unstructured retreat. The weekend I visited, they hosted a Spanish-speaking Marriage Encounter retreat. Holy Cross is also home to art workshops, 12-step programs, Elderhostel (an educational adventure group for the 55-and-over crowd), Catholic and non-Catholic retreat groups, and university and public school planning and training seminars. In addition, they offer a special ministry to cancer patients, providing rooms and meals to those who must travel to Las Cruces for chemotherapy.

Other Retreats

Los Olmos Guest Ranch, Glenwood, 505-539-2311

Sacred Places

77. The Catwalk

Glenwood Chamber of Commerce
P.O. Box 183
Glenwood, NM 88039
505-539-2711

*I*n 1859, gold was discovered in the Mogollon mountains. To ensure maintenance on the streamside pipelines that serviced the mill and town of Graham, the first catwalk was constructed 20 years later. (The hike was called a catwalk because you needed the footwork skill of a cat to maneuver up the pipes.) At the present-day site of picnic area, you can still see the remains of this old catwalk in the form of bent pipeline, large iron bolts, and concrete.

In the 1960s, the Forest Service constructed the catwalk you traverse today; it is now designated a National Recreation Trail.

This is a rousing hike, about 20 feet above Whitewater Creek through a deep gorge. Rock walls tower over 1,000 feet above you, while water swirls and crashes below. All this occurs amidst magnificent, white-barked

Location: 70 miles northwest of Silver City.

Description: A spectacular catwalk hike up a narrow whitewater gorge.

Spiritual Significance: River, rock, ancient Apache lands, negative ions galore.

Solitude Rating: ★★★★

How to get there: Take US 180 to Glenwood. On the north side of town, turn east onto NM 174, Catwalk Road.

Accessibility from highway: Easy.

Facilities: Developed picnic area at the trailhead.

Fee Area: No.

sycamores with thick limbs that crawl and climb and majestic Douglas firs that reach for the canyon rim. Cottonwoods, oaks, and black walnuts line the darkened riverbank. It feels like magic as you make your way up the steep, narrow canyon, across bridges and along railed walkways that hug the rock.

This is one walk you definitely want to take in the off-season. Perhaps during the rebirth of spring, amidst wild flowers, fresh green leaves, and the crystal-cold water runoff from the mountains. Or, perhaps you prefer the luminescent colors of dying autumn, when the sycamores and maples turn crimson. If you go during these times, on a weekday, you will most assuredly have the place to yourself. For even more solitude, continue beyond the heavily used catwalk onto Trail 207, which heads up the rock at the front end of the final suspension bridge. After approximately 2 miles you come to the South Fork Trail 212. If you turn right and continue up the south fork, you are greeted by big-tooth maples and beautiful, grassy resting and camping spots.

I walked the catwalk on a foggy, damp autumn day. I love fog—it creates a mood like no other weather and this day was no exception. The canyon was full of mist and mystery. All was pewter, as the smooth rock arches and massive old boulders took on a new vibrancy, as if they wanted to share their tales of the times when Gerónimo and Butch Cassidy hid among their shadows and bodies were swept away by roaring waters.

> Deep is calling on deep, in the roar of waters;
> your torrents and all your waves swept over me.
>
> —Psalm 42

78. Datil Well Woodlands

BLM Datil Well National Recreation Area
198 Neal Ave.
Socorro, NM 87801
505-835-0412
www.publiclands.org

As poet Robert Graves, author of *The White Goddess,* has so well expressed, trees have long been believed to be the special spirits of places. Myths around the world speak of a Tree of Life or World Tree that was, in some way, involved with the creation of the universe and the origin of humanity. Trees were worshipped and recognized for all their special gifts upon which humans depended: food, medicines, boats, fire, carts, clothing, fuel. Indeed, trees were thought to be a conscious piece of the living web of earth.

This forest is one of those places where you feel it is so. Perhaps it's the humongous size of the alligator juniper. Perhaps it's the variety in their "voices" as the wind passes through their innumerable leaves and needles. This forest is a convergence of tree spirits that lifts you above the mundane and into the place of play and smiles.

Once on the path, bear right whenever you come to a junction. These paths are well-marked and relatively easy, taking you through piñon-juniper woodlands and the lonesome call of the Townsend's solitaire. Look for their gray, streamlined bodies on the tops of the trees. Once you pass through the second wooden, zigzag gate, you begin your entrance into the special canyon of old spirits: Emory oak, Gambel oak, Arizona cypress, ponderosa pine, one-seed juniper, alligator juniper, and Rocky Mountain juniper. What are they all doing in one place? Walk among them, sit, and listen. But do not pass up this opportunity to feel their presence. This place and these spirits will soothe

Location: 1 mile west of Datil.

Description: Well-marked trails through gentle hills and forests comprised of trees on their farthest boundaries, making for an unusual and fascinating woodland community.

Spiritual Significance: Forest, rock, splendiferous birdsong, coyote, walking meditation, convergence.

Solitude Rating: ★★★★★

How to get there: From Datil, go west on US 60 for 0.8 mile. Turn left onto a well-marked gravel road that directs you to Datil Well Campground. A marked trail begins at campsite 10. Or, to avoid the campground, drive past the campground entrance, down the road a short ways, and watch for the trail to cross the gravel road. Pull over, park, and begin the walk from here.

Accessibility from highway: Easy.

Facilities: Campground, water, restrooms, picnic area.

Fee Area: Yes, in campground. None to hike.

and relax and help bring forth your intent. Nuthatch, chickadee. All converge. Here. With you.

Once you get your feet back under you, continue up the trail, again bearing right at the junctions (this takes you on the outer loop of the trail, about 3 miles round-trip). Your next destination is Rocky Point, a primo meditation spot. Here you sit amidst large rocks with a view of the spacious San Agustin Plains, upon boulders covered with ancient lichens of luminescent lime green, golds, browns, and oranges.

While I was here, it started to rain, adding another layer of beauty and silence to an already sanctified landscape. I heard a coyote "yip" in the distance, and smiled and stopped in my tracks, ever so glad to hear an old friend. When I came to a split in the trail, I went left, thinking it would take me back to the trailhead. Instead, it took me in a circle and dropped me back where I'd made my mistake—and where a fresh pile of coyote scat sat right in the middle of the trail.

Not many people come to this place. The terrain is not spectacular; there are no gushing mountain streams, no steep, craggy mountains. The message of this place is its quiet simplicity amidst awesome diversity. An unusual convergence of spirit, rock, tree—and for those who get too comfortable—coyote.

79. Gila Cliff Dwellings

Gila Cliff Dwellings National Monument
HC 68, Box 100
Silver City, NM 88061
505-536-9461
www.nps.gov/gicl

$\mathcal{T}$he streamside, canyon walk into the cliff dwellings is simply sublime. The trail is 1 mile round-trip, with a steep uphill section to the cliffs on a dirt trail with no railings (wear shoes with good traction). But the hike is worth it—the area bursts with green, and like the ruins above you, is full of the silence of the ancient ones. The walk is slow and serene, as you continue up and up, to

Location: 44 miles north of Silver City.

Description: An awe-inspiring ancient Pueblo village of the Mogollon culture from around A.D. 1280. The cliff dwellings are located in the Gila National Forest at the edge of the Gila Wilderness Area.

Spiritual Significance: Caves, ruins, river.

Solitude Rating: ★★

How to get there: Take NM 15 north from Silver City. Although the distance is only 44 miles, the paved road is very tight and winding, making the travel time from Silver City more than 2 hours. Give yourself plenty of time and breaks so you don't arrive exhausted. This is not a road on which you want to be in a hurry.

Accessibility from highway: Fair.

Facilities: Visitor center, picnic areas, and camping. No trash containers—be prepared to pack out all garbage. Overnight lodging, a convenience store, and gas are available in the nearby town of Gila Hot Springs.

Fee Area: Yes.

the cliffs above. The journey offers a glimpse into the lives lived here, as the people came down to this stream to collect water and carry it up to their homes high above.

The south-facing cliff above you features seven natural caves. In all, their dwellings totaled around 40 rooms. The Mogollon people probably came to this specific location and constructed these homes during the great drought, around A.D. 1270. Whatever their motivation, they chose well—the south-facing cliffs offered winter sun, while the Gila River offered year-round water, lush vegetation, and many game animals.

This is a place of old, old spirits. Of people who worked the land and traded with their neighbors. A bison scraper from the eastern plains and macaw feathers from Mexico were found here. The mystery and beauty transports you to an earlier day, when winds roared and people huddled around their winter fires.

The Mogollon lived here for about 100 years before moving on, in the early 1300s. No one knows their full story. The reason for their departure is a mystery, but it's believed that they traveled to the pueblos on the Rio Grande.

80. Gila Riparian Preserve

New Mexico Nature Conservancy
Cliff, NM 88028
505-988-3867
www.tnc.org/infield/state/newmex/preserves/gila.htm

With lush woodlands, rock bluffs, and a river that runs through, it doesn't get much better than this—until you add solitude and birdsong. One-third of all bird species in North America have been sighted in this preserve. If birds soothe your spirit, then this is a special place for you.

Location: 28 miles west of Silver City in the Gila River Valley.

Description: A 7,308-acre preserve featuring prime riparian habitat that offers fabulous wildlife watching, river terrain, and rich woodlands.

Spiritual Significance: River, forest, bird oasis, historic Apache lands.

Solitude Rating: ★★★★★

How to get there: Take US 180 to the town of Cliff, which is 28 miles west of Silver City. At Cliff, turn north onto NM 293. Follow this road, which turns to gravel, about 7 miles into the Gila National Forest. Bear left when you drop into the riverbed area. The entrance to the preserve is gated to cars, but there is an opening to walk through. Look for the large rock piles that mark the spot. Cross the river and look off straight ahead, slightly to your right, and you will see another gate that marks the nature preserve.

Accessibility from highway: Fair.

Facilities: Primitive camping area on the forest lands adjacent to the preserve.

Fee Area: No.

If a variety of birds excites you, then there's no question that you must walk these lands, which include the endangered Gila woodpecker and the southwestern willow flycatcher.

Sit and soak in the beauty and song of this area. The ancient Gila River that rolls past you is the last major free-flowing river in New Mexico. Wild and free, her regular floods replenish the lands with soil and seed, producing the most diverse deciduous broadleaf woodland in New Mexico, including oaks, sycamores, cottonwoods, and black walnuts. Watch the birds fly and hear them call—blue grosbeaks, Scott's orioles, warblers, elf owls, tanagers, flickers, and cardinals.

Brilliant wings that sweep on high, blessed sanctuary of earth and sky.

81. Kneeling Nun Mountain

East of Hanover

$\mathcal{T}$he little town of Santa Rita doesn't exist anymore, subsumed by the gargantuan mine that now bears the village's name. According to Phelps Dodge Mining Co. (the owners of the Santa Rita Mine and Kneeling Nun Mountain), the mine extracted 317 million pounds of copper in 1998. Despite the earth-moving commotion of humankind, the kneeling nun still bows at the head of her mountain. Her legends date back to the time of the Aztecs and to the Conquistadors when they first traveled north. She has seen it all from her wondrous vantage point, as she looks over the land known for its purest copper. She watched as the Indians, Spanish, and later the Anglo corporations, moved in and found ways to extract the valuable mineral.

You see her kneeling, above the mine, as if to pray and bless this place of ancient removal. The miners believed she was their guardian, and people say some workers refused to work in the Santa Rita Pit unless they were able to do so within her protective view. Another story tells of a nun, native to the area, who nursed an injured Spanish soldier back to health. Despite her vows of chastity, she fell in love with him, was cast from her convent, and turned to stone.

Whatever the tale, you feel her pervasive presence. She welcomes human arrival and has been standing high above all ever since. Through bloodshed, deceit, and the ambush murder of Apache chief Juan José. Through greed, danger, and the growth of the bustling town of Santa Rita. And through the ravenous pit before her that may threaten her very existence. Many claim continued blasting at the mine weakens her while growing piles of tailings obscure and eliminate public views. In 1998, a coalition of the United Steelworkers Local 890, the National Congress of American Indians, the Mexicano-Chicano Chamber of Commerce, the National Wildlife Federation, and 8,000 citizens signed petitions to include Kneeling Nun Mountain as part of the National Park System. They also asked for her protection under the Antiquities and National Historic Preservation Act, seeking to gain safe, public access to her sacred image. Progress is slow, but it does appear that encroachment upon the hem of her skirt may halt.

Location: Just off NM 152 to the south, about 18 miles east of Silver City.

Description: A natural rock formation resembling a kneeling nun that is a source of spiritual inspiration and protection.

Spiritual Significance: Ancient spiritual landmark.

Solitude Rating: ★

How to get there: Drive east from Silver City on US 180. When you reach NM 152, go east. You will see the monolith at the edge of a table mountain, just above the Chino Mine and the famous Santa Rita pit.

Accessibility from highway: View from highway only, a good distance away.

Facilities: None.

Fee Area: No.

82. La Cueva

BLM Dripping Springs Natural Area
1800 Marquess
Las Cruces, NM 88005
505-522-1219

*A*gostini Justiniani, the spiritual pilgrim who supposedly studied for the priesthood in his homeland of Italy but refused his vows, returns to us through this site. Known as Giovanni Agostini when he lived near Las Vegas, N.M., in the 1860s, he left his cave on Tecolote Mountain, now known as Hermit Peak. Repeating his past travels, he walked with a wagon train, this time to Mesilla. From Mesilla, a small town just outside Las Cruces, Agostini walked to San Antonio, Texas, and then into Juarez, Mexico, where he stayed in a cave for awhile. Agostini returned to Mesilla and made plans to live at La Cueva. To ease his friends' fears that his plans might put him in danger, he told them he would make a fire in front of his cave every Friday

Location: In the Organ Mountains, 9 miles east of Las Cruces.

Description: A rock shelter used during the prehistoric Jornada Mogollon cultures and more recently home to El Ermitaño, the hermit (see Hermit Peak, page 166).

Spiritual Significance: Desert, mountain, cave, ancient Indian dwelling, home to spiritual ascetic, Agostini Justiniani.

Solitude Rating: ★★

How to get there: Drive east from Las Cruces on University Avenue, which becomes Dripping Springs Road, eventually turning from pavement to dirt. Follow the signs to Dripping Springs and the A.B. Cox Visitor Center. You can access the turnoff for La Cueva from the main visitor center or from the picnic and parking area that branches to your left as you enter the developed area. From the Cox Visitor Center, you can also hike to Dripping Springs Natural Area (1.5 miles, one way).

Accessibility from highway: Fair.

Facilities: Picnic area, campground, water, bathrooms, visitors' center.

Fee area: Yes.

evening to let them know all was well. In the spring Easter season of the same year, the fire failed to appear. Antonio Garcia, who had taken the sick to El Ermitaño to be healed, went up the mountain to check on the Hermit. Garcia found the hermit lying face down on his crucifix, wearing a penitential metal girdle full of spikes, with a knife in his back.

When you stand in this cave, it's easy to see why it has attracted those seeking shelter from the earliest of times. The wide, gaping cave, which goes back about 30 feet into the rock cliff, has a southern exposure and is near a spring and a stream. Plus, it's barely visible from a distance. Archeologists have determined that this cave was occupied from around 5000 B.C. until the arrival of the Europeans.

Numerous spiritual hermits, many of whom lived in caves, are known to us today through their sainthood: Saint Francis, Saint Anthony of the Desert, Saint Benedict, Saint Paul, and Mary Magdalene. El Ermitaño never achieved such public status, but wherever he roamed he became known for his special healing powers and deep religious conviction.

A portrait of the hermit hangs in the small, homey Gadston Museum in La Mesilla. Here, you can also see a ring he wore, his rosary, and his diary. El Ermitaño, devout man of penance, came to this house to lecture. He is buried just a few blocks away in the San Albino cemetery at the south end of Calle de Guadalupe.

83. Lady on the Mountain

Magdalena

D.H. Lawrence, who wrote extensively of the lands of New Mexico, refers to Mary Magdalene as the Priestess Isis in *The Man Who Died*. Indeed, her mystical, potent occurrence throughout time has been of awesome proportions. After his resurrection, Jesus appeared first to her (Mark 16:9). Legends say she is the woman who carried perfume in an alabaster vase. She anointed the feet of Jesus with her tears and wiped them with her long, ravishing hair. Jesus referred to Mary Magdalene as "the Apostle" to his own Apostles and "the Woman Who Knew the All." She sat next to him, and received private teachings from him. Ultimately, his words to her, "Go in peace," were indelibly written upon her heart and into the teachings of her life. She eventually immigrated to what is now France and lived 40 miles from Marseilles. Here, she dwelled in a sacred

Location: On the side of Magdalena Mountain outside the town of Magdalena.

Description: The centuries-old natural rock image of Saint Mary Magdalene is an ancient sacred refuge for those seeking protection.

Spiritual Significance: Mountain, spiritual image, miracle.

Solitude Rating: ★★★★★

How to get there: Magdalena is located on US 60, west of Socorro. From the village of Magdalena, turn south onto Kelly Road next to the Ranger Station. Magdalena Mountain is the peak to the left of the M-shaped mountain. As you drive south, you will see the image of Mary Magdalene on the east face of the mountain.

Accessibility from highway: View from highway only.

Facilities: In Magdalena.

Fee Area: No.

cave at St. Baume (Holy Tree), where it is said she lived like a mystic for 30 years without food or water, surviving solely on the songs of angels. Whatever images her name and visage incites, there is no doubt she was an ancient woman of power, so potent that generations of people have seen her image in the rock slide formation that covers a large portion of the east slope of Magdalena Mountain.

As with many places mentioned in this book, tales buzz 'round like bees to honey. This mountain is not without its miracle story, as the face of Mary Magdalene is said to have suddenly appeared when a group of Mexican people were attacked by Apaches on the mountain. Her shocking appearance frightened the attackers away, saving the lives of the people. Or, perhaps the origin is as simple as an early Spanish priest seeing her image and naming the mountain in her honor. This place is supposedly still held sacred by many Native Americans, who in the past sought Mary Magdalene's safety from attacks by other tribes.

Pull over anywhere, stand before her mountain on the high desert, and gaze upon her image. Saint Mary Magdalene casts her spell downward upon the landscape and over your body. "Go in peace," she whispers from afar.

84. Pancho Villa Memorial

Pancho Villa State Park
P.O. Box 224
Junction of NM 9 & 11
Columbus, NM 88029
505-531-2711

The stories of Old Mexico and New Mexico were tightly intertwined for oh-so-many centuries. Ancient Indian trails and trade knew no borders between north and south. El Camino Real from Mexico City provided the goods for New Mexico's settlement, as well as passageway for the first

Franciscan priests who traveled to the new world to convert the Indian population. When the United States set her sights on the territory of New Mexico, Old Mexico did not look kindly, as the War of 1848 showed. Due to lingering mistrust, New Mexico did not become the 47th state until 1912.

This site is important for all it brings to history and spirit. Pancho Villa, a revolutionary, was born in 1877 in the Mexican state of Durango. His beginnings were more outlaw than military man—at age 16 he became a murderer and fugitive when he avenged the rape of his sister. But history was good to Pancho, who was to become one of the greatest members of the revolutionary army, on behalf of the poor and downtrodden people of Mexico. The revolutionary armies were successful in ending the brutal dictatorship of Porfirio Diaz in 1910, and in making Francisco Madero, leader of the popular revolt, the provisional president of Mexico. Madero, however, was executed by General Huerta and the bloody battles continued. President Woodrow Wilson, once a friend to Villa, took steps to undermine him. Some say this is why Villa invaded Columbus on an early March morning in 1916, but others say it was because a Columbus townsman sold Villa bad ammunition. There are accounts of the raiding soldiers asking for this man, who happened to be out of town.

Whatever the motivation, it is clear that Villa's army caught the United States Army sleeping, literally and figuratively. The soldiers of Camp Furlong,

Location: 32 miles south of Deming.

Description: The site of the last foreign invasion into the United States, where Mexican revolutionary General Francisco Pancho Villa crossed the international boundary and raided the town of Columbus on March 9, 1916. A wonderful, informative visitor center offers a film.

Spiritual Significance: Memorial, desert botanical gardens.

Solitude Rating: ★★

How to get there: From Deming, travel south on NM 11. Once in the small town of Columbus, you will see the park and can drive straight to it. The park is on your right, just past the small town plaza on your left.

Accessibility from highway: Easy.

Facilities: In the town of Columbus. Extensive campground on the state park grounds, water, visitor center.

Fee Area: Yes.

stationed in Columbus, were in disarray when the attack began and their guns were locked safely away...from themselves. Singing "La Cucaracha" and yelling "Viva Mexico," 500 of Villa's troops strode down the streets. Described as "poorly dressed but heavily armed," they looted, burned, and shot up the town. By daylight, the revolutionaries were gone, leaving 108 dead, including 10 civilians.

On March 16, 1916, General Jack Pershing arrived in Columbus and set up camp. With 10,000 men, he traveled 500 miles into Mexico in search of Pancho Villa. The final cavalry action of the U.S. Army, it was the first time cars were used in military action and the first time an airplane was used for reconnaissance. The action also signaled the advent of photojournalism, attracting the likes of John Reed of the *New York World,* Floyd Gibbons of the *Chicago Tribune,* and Alfred Henry Lewis of Hearst News Service.

The United States' mighty force, akin to an elephant rumbling down the dusty roads, did not find Pancho Villa, a.k.a. The Jackrabbit. After crossing into Mexico and searching for 11 months, they returned to Columbus in February of 1917.

Every year, on March 9, Columbus hosts a Memorial Service in memory of raid day. They also host a Fiesta de Amistad, or Friendship Festival, an international event to promote friendship and good will between the two countries. The festival includes more than 40 Mexican horseback riders who ride from Janos, Mexico, to Columbus, in a deeply moving display.

The little lady who hosts the visitor center describes mixed responses regarding the name of this park and memorial. Americans wonder why the park is named for Pancho Villa, the enemy. And Mexicans want to know why there isn't a memorial to the Villa-istas who were shot and hung.

I stand on lonely Coote's hill, the American flag waving above me. The flat, hot desert plains, from which Villa and his troops materialized, extend before me. I feel awash in the contradictions and histories of two nations that are anything but simple.

Pancho Villa was a man who should not be forgotten. True revolutionaries come from the earth, and although their means are often violent, they act on behalf of the powerless. How can powerful intentions on behalf of the disenfranchised not be considered sacred?

At the base of Coote's Hill is a plaque from the State of New Mexico that commemorates peace between the two neighboring nations. The way in which one acknowledges and honors defeat is one true test of spiritual strength.

85. Very Large Array (VLA)

National Radio Astronomy Observatory
P.O. Box 0
Socorro, NM 87801
www.aoc.nrao.edu/vla/html/vlahome.shtml

*T*hey perch mightily on the Plains of San Agustin, amidst old, dilapidated farm buildings and windmills that still go 'round. The first time you see these monstrous, striking, white metal antennae, you can't quite believe your eyes. They are at once frightening and majestic. And you are drawn to know more.

If you saw the movie *Contact* with Jodie Foster, you already have an idea of the immensity and mystery of this site. Astronomer Carl Sagan's story of outer space contact was filmed here. Appropriate enough for this site that "listens" to outer space 24 hours a day, every day of the year. The lonely, sparse San Agustin Plains, home to rattlesnakes and scorpions, share the name of the austere saint, known for solitary confrontations with the

Location: 20 miles west of Magdalena in the oceanic San Agustin Plains.

Description: The most powerful outer space telescope in the world with 27 large dish antennae, each 94 feet tall in locations spanning 22 miles, at an altitude of 7,000 feet. Visitor center with film and a self-guided walking tour. Open daily, 8:30 a.m. to sunset.

Spiritual Significance: Cosmic communications, space exploration and discoveries.

Solitude Rating: ★★

How to get there: From Magdalena, travel 20 miles west on US 60 until you reach the turnoff for the VLA. Turn south on NM 52, and then turn right onto NM 166, which takes you into the visitor center.

Accessibility from highway: Easy.

Facilities: Water and bathrooms at visitor center.

Fee Area: No.

divine. And so it is these 27 antennae seek solitary confrontation of a different nature, "seeing" matter between stars where humans once believed there were vacuums, and recording quasars from distant galaxies.

The VLA is the most powerful radio telescope in the world. It captures radio signals from outer space and sends them to a central location where computers translate them into detailed pictures. In a sense, it is a time machine, creating images of events that took place millions of years ago. That's how long it took for the signal from the stars and galaxies beyond to reach VLA's ears. It is almost more than the mind can grasp. From this VLA have come images of distant gamma ray explosions on the outer edge of the universe and the massive black hole that fuels our galaxy and sends our imaginations reeling. The color photos in the visitor center stop you in your tracks.

The spiritual implications of this site are many, for some olden pueblo peoples believe their ancestors came from the stars. The VLA exquisitely symbolizes our earthbound existence and its celestial context. Here we are, human beings made from the same elements that are found in the stars, twirling around on our spiral galaxy known as the Milky Way.

The old ones say if we can find peace and wonder in the space between the stars, then we will understand our place among them. From the ancient inland sea of San Agustin, this spectacle of telescope brings us ever closer to our "home" from far away.

Spiritual Events

86. Dia de los Muertos Celebration, Calavera Coalition

October 31–November 2
On the plaza, Mesilla

*I*n New Mexico, Dia de los Muertos (The Day of the Dead) on Nov. 2 is a momentous time of remembrance. Of Mexican origins, the Day of the Dead blends with the popular United States holiday known as Halloween, and the Catholic-rooted All Saints Day and All Souls Day. Including the days from Oct. 31 through Nov. 2, the celebration offers a rich experience of traditions and ritual, based on the belief that the veil between the living and the dead is thinnest at this time of year. In short, communication with the spirits of the dead is easy—visitations are not only common, they're expected!

Outside New Mexico and Old Mexico, most people celebrate Halloween on Oct. 31. Most Halloween traditions are based in the ancient Celtic harvest festival known as Samhain (pronounced sow-wen), when people tried to appease the souls of the dead, who can cause great havoc. Jack-o'-lanterns were actually lanterns, to light the way and keep one safe, and treats were actually used to prevent the trick.

Here in New Mexico, it's a very different story. Once the trick-or-treaters come and go and the costumes are packed away, attention focuses on rituals that go back to the time when indigenous peoples practiced ancient rites that mocked and celebrated death. Instead of fear and mourning, this time honors the return of spirits departed, reminding us of our own eventual demise. This is the time when the dead return home to visit loved ones and feast on their favorite foods. One Pueblo tribe thoroughly cleans their homes in preparation for the spirits. Then, they cook the favorite meals of the departed and place them on their graves.

The Hispanic celebration includes the creation of simple or elaborate altars with *ofrendas* (offerings), which include the deceased's favorite foods, yellow marigolds (a symbol of death), *pan de muerto* (bread of death), pictures, toys, and other symbolic offerings. Candles are lit on the altars, to help the returning souls find their way back. Many families gather to clean the cemeteries and decorate the graves of their loved ones with marigolds. Sometimes, headstones are painted and candles are lit, a mysterious and beautiful sight. In the old tradition of Mexico, families bring toys for dead children and tequila and cigarettes for adults. Some stay at the cemetery all day, sit on blankets next to the graves, and eat the favorite foods of their beloved or consume a sugar skull with the name of the departed written on it.

The Dia de los Muertos celebration in Mesilla, outside Las Cruces, is one of the most varied, fun, and meaningful in New Mexico. Although specifics may change, the Calavera Coalition's event follows a general outline of celebration and festival that spans several days and includes altar workshops, a *calavera* (skull) piñata, lively music, a talk on the history of Dia de los Muertos, a Dance of Death, and, on Nov. 2, a candlelight procession with *El Gigante* (the giant).

The Spaniards were appalled when they first came across the Aztec and other Mesoamerican peoples using human skulls to honor the dead in a month-long ritual. Believing that death was the end of life, this celebration brought the Spaniards "head to head" with those who viewed death as a continuation of life. Mictecacihuatl, a goddess who died at birth and is known as Lady of the Dead, presided over all events.

It is her I imagine when I read of the *angelitos*, "little angels," the children who have died and now follow a path of saffron marigolds home, where their families have made altars of milk, sweet tamales, sugar *calaveras*, and *pan de muerto*—just for them.

As the Calavera Coalition so aptly reminds us through their wondrous celebration of tradition: *Recordar es Vivir!* "To remember is to live." For information, call Mesilla Visitor's Center, 505-647-9698, Town Hall, 505-524-3262, or Las Cruces Chamber of Commerce, 505-524-1968.

87. Mass Ascension, Water Birds

November–February
Bosque del Apache National Wildlife Refuge
South of San Antonio

*I*t didn't matter who I asked—whether a Native American medicine woman or a historian of New Mexico—when I surveyed my friends about sacred places and events in New Mexico, this site came up repeatedly. There is simply nothing like the mass ascension of tens of thousands of ducks, geese, and cranes, off waters close enough to feel their wing beats. Your heart takes flight right along with them, and you are never quite the same.

It is winter at the Bosque del Apache (Woods of the Apache), so named for the Apache Indians who regularly camped along the Rio Grande forest. Just before sunlight scrapes the waters, you hear the squawking of ducks, the honking of geese, and the prehistoric call of the sandhill crane. The sun cracks the horizon, something moves—perhaps a coyote, perhaps a reed upon the water—and the birds lift off and you are overtaken by a roar of wings and the gush of a sudden breath. In the evening, you see wave upon wave of geese and cranes returning to their watery roosts. This is why Bosque is known as the most spectacular refuge in North America.

The mass ascension of these snow geese and other water birds takes place south of San Antonio from November to February. Photo by Wendy Shattil.

Winter is prime time for the mass ascensions of Arctic geese and sandhill cranes. At dawn or dusk, in the trees, above you in the sky, or flying low in search of food, you'll see bald eagles, northern harriers, and red-tailed hawks. On the waters, you'll spot Canada geese, northern shovelers, mallards, cormorants, and pintail ducks. Meanwhile, mule deer, coyotes, and perhaps pheasants, turkeys, and roadrunners traipse the land.

It is awesome to think what these birds and their ancestors have seen on these waters. More than 700 years ago, the Piro Indians lived here, farmed, and hunted wildlife. In the late 16th century, El Camino Real, the Royal Road between Mexico City and Santa Fe, carried trade along the Rio, a major element of development of the New World. Remnants of this history are protected within the Bosque Refuge boundaries.

The Bosque del Apache National Wildlife Refuge was established in 1939 to provide safe breeding grounds for migratory birds and other wildlife. Today, it provides food, water, and shelter for wildlife and works diligently to return the native bosque cottonwoods and willows to the Rio Grande area.

The Bosque del Apache National Wildlife Refuge offers nature trails, a picnic area near the visitor center (or you can eat your picnic at your vehicle along the tour route), and a wilderness area of 30,000 acres.

The Bosque is off I-25 midway between Albuquerque and Las Cruces. Drive 8 miles south from Socorro to Exit 139. Go east 0.25 mile on US 380 to the flashing signal at San Antonio, N.M., and turn right onto Old Highway (NM) 1. Continue south 9 miles to the visitor center. There is no camping. It opens an hour before sunrise and closes an hour after sundown, every day of the year. Prime time is dawn or dusk, November through February. For information, call 505-835-1828, or check out their website at www.friendsofthebosque.org.

88. Pilgrimage in Honor of La Virgen de Guadalupe

December 9–12

Tortugas

To know and understand New Mexico is first to know and understand her sacred Guadalupe. Protectress of New Mexico, she is known by many names: The Virgin Mary of Guadalupe, Our Lady of Guadalupe, La Morena, La Morenita, La Madrecita, The Dark Virgin, La Virgen de Tepeyac, Nuestra Señora, La Virgen de Guadalupe, and Tonantzin, "Our Mother." Her image is seen throughout New Mexico, in some places that you'd expect, such as churches, candles, and personal home altars—and on places you might not predict, such as wall murals, car hoods, tiles, T-shirts, and keychains.

Guadalupe first appeared to a humble Aztec peasant, Juan Diego, in 1531 on the Aztec hill of Tepeyac (now the eastern edge of Mexico City). To him, she most likely would have been Tequatlanopeuh, "She Whose Origins Were in the Rocky Summit." She spoke not in Spanish, but in his native Nahuatl tongue. She asked him to build her a shrine on the same spot where a temple once stood to the Aztecan goddess, Tonantzin, which was destroyed by Cortez. Four times she appeared to Juan Diego, four being the sacred number of completion, representing air, earth, water, and fire. Her visits were filled with the humbling power of miracle. She caused roses to grow atop the rocky, barren Tepeyac in the dead of winter, and then she helped Juan to pick them. Her image appeared miraculously upon Juan Diego's cactus-fiber cloak. Her fifth appearance, which would have represented the "center" to the indigenous sacred circle, was her healing visitation to Juan Diego's ailing uncle.

Guadalupe, adorned with the sun, standing upon the moon with a crown of 12 stars, has since come to represent the ultimate Mother, as signified in this prayer:

> Am I not here, Your Mother?
> Are you not under my shadow and protection?
> Am I not your foundation of life?
> Are you not in the folds of my mantle, in the crossing of my arms?
> Is there anything else you need?

Since then, this indigenous goddess has embraced the contradictions and complexities of the old and new worlds, the conquerors and the conquered. She is the ultimate Mother, Patroness of Mexican and Native American peoples.

And so it is that her devotees gather and celebrate her coming. For more than 150 years, public pilgrimages have been held in her honor, over rocky, thorn-filled desert terrain, through snow, under unforgiving sun. Her New Mexico gatherings are like none other. While traditional Christian pilgrimages usually involve a visit to holy sites, graves, or places of suffering, the destination of New Mexico pilgrims is commonly a hilltop and/or a sanctuary. Where Guadalupe is concerned, the hilltop is symbolic of Tepeyac Hill, and a pilgrimage in her name is not as much a solemn procession as a quest that involves a promise or vow.

The Tortugas pilgrimage, thought to be the oldest in New Mexico, originated after the first settlement there in the 1840s. The Tortugas pueblo, founded in 1852, is a mix of indigenous peoples who have intermarried with Hispanic and Mexican peoples. Thus, their celebration is a fascinating meld of the traditions and customs of the Hispanics and Native Americans of the El Paso, Texas area, as well as of past and recent customs of Mexico. Once a year, commencing on the evening of Dec. 10, a three-day celebration, called a Triduum, begins in honor of Our Lady of Guadalupe. On Dec. 10 after sunset, a processional, prayers, and dancing begin and bonfires are lit in her honor. Many stay up the entire night. The following day, Dec. 11, begins in the early morning darkness with the ceremony known as La Alba, meaning "dawn." A processional moves her to Our Lady of Guadalupe Church, under the watchful eye of men who fire guns to ward off evil spirits. Between 6 and 7 a.m., you make your way to La Casa del Pueblo and sign in for the pilgrimage, buy a candle to carry to the top of the mountain, and leave a donation to those who have worked so hard, including Los Indigenes de Nuestra Señora de Guadalupe, the group dedicated to preserving the traditional Pueblo customs. Sign-in is followed by a procession to Our Lady of Guadalupe Church, where everyone enters (women first, then men), approaches Nuestra Señora to kneel, pray, or kiss, then departs through a side door. A double line is formed outside on the dirt dancing grounds, one line of women and one of men. They form a sacred circle, where ritual tobacco smoke carries the prayers to the four directions, and you are reminded that you are a part of a 150-year tradition.

The journey is approximately 3.5 miles from the village to the summit. The final 0.5 mile up the mountain is steep and rocky. Once you arrive at the mountain's base, you pick your route, walk, pray, and rest. Continue until you reach the top, adorned with colorful altars to Guadalupe. Here you approach her, light your candle, and place it on the altar as you give thanks, pray, and perhaps join many others and weep your great release. Everyone feels the glory of their great walk. Families cook food over open fires, while others gather in circles and make exquisitely beautiful staffs called *quiotes* from yucca blossoms and stems. At 11 a.m., the bishop conducts a Mass. Some leave the mountain following the Mass, departing down the steep trail, staff in hand. But many stay until after dark, when fires are set, up and down the mountain, to light the way for the Virgin to follow the same route as her people and enter the pueblo for her annual visit.

The next morning is Dec. 12, the official Feast Day of Our Lady of Guadalupe, when celebration breaks forth into outright joy. The day is full of dances in her honor. Among the vibrant and shimmering costumes, you see a lot of red, scarlet, and crimson—the colors that symbolize life and vitality. It feels as if the energy will never, never die.

And so it is, that for three days in December, the imperfect hill strewn with broken glass, gouged with abandoned quarries, pitted with bullets, and dotted with sprouting antennas, forgets its blemishes. For one celebration, you see only her sharp rocks and blessed trails. For one trip, you focus only on the ground beneath your feet, as you climb, step by step, to the sacred top. When, in the name of Our Lady of Guadalupe, the hill known as "A" Mountain to some (for the home-team Aggies), and Tortugas (tortoises) to others, becomes the holy, symbolic Tepeyac.

Call 505-526-8171 for information.

Opposite: An image of Our Lady of Guadalupe at Pecos Abbey (Our Lady of Guadalupe Benedictine Abbey).

Appendix A

Historical Time Line of New Mexico

12,000–10,000 B.C. ....Sandía people, the earliest evidence of human existence in New Mexico.

10,000–9000 B.C. ....Clovis peoples hunt mammoth and bison.

9000–8000 B.C. ....Folsom peoples throughout the Southwest.

10,000–500 B.C. ....Cochise people, earliest evidence of agriculture in the Southwest.

A.D. 1–700 ....Anasazi basketmakers and weavers.

A.D. 700–1300 ....Anasazi Pueblo culture climaxes with Chaco Civilization.

A.D. 300–1400 ....Mogollon culture, pottery as high art.

A.D. 1200–1500 ....Pueblo Indians settle along the Rio Grande.

1536 ....Cabeza de Vaca and others reach Mexico and possibly southern New Mexico; the rumor of the Seven Cities of Cibola is born.

1540–42 ....Francisco Coronado travels in the area from Kansas to Grand Canyon.

1598 ....Juan de Oñate establishes first Spanish capitol at Tewa village of Ohkay (Ohke), north of present day Española.

This Navajo hogan still stands strong after many years.

A picturesque church in Lumberton rises against a bright blue backdrop.

Early 1600s .... Camino Real becomes major trade and colonization route between Mexico City and Santa Fe, with later extension to Taos.

1608 .... Oñate removed as governor and returned to Mexico City to be tried for mistreatment of Indians and abuse of power.

1609 .... Santa Fe established as capitol.

1680 .... By 1680, 80 Catholic Missions exist around the state. Pueblo Indian Revolt begins, led by Popay and planned inside the Taos Pueblo; all missions burned and destroyed; church leaders murdered; surviving Spanish colonists flee to El Paso del Norte.

Late 1600s .... The Navajo, Apache, and Comanche begin raids against Pueblo Indians.

1692 .... Spanish recolonization of Santa Fe by Don Diego de Vargas and conquest of New Mexico.

1706 .... Albuquerque founded.

1807 .... Zebulon Pike leads first Anglo-American expedition into New Mexico.

1821 .... Mexico declares independence from Spain.

1826 .... Kit Carson arrives in Taos; settles at present museum site in 1843.

1837 .... Chimayo Revolt against Mexican taxation.

1846 .... Mexican-American War. New Mexico annexed to the United States.

1847 .... Taos Rebellion against U.S. military presence.

1848 .... Treaty of Guadalupe Hidalgo ends Mexican-American War.

1850	New Mexico (which then included the lands of Arizona and parts of Utah, Colorado, and Nevada) is designated a U.S. territory.
1854	Gadsen Purchase adds 45,000 square miles of Mexican lands to New Mexico territory.
1861	Confederates invade New Mexico. La Mesilla declared capitol of Confederate Territory.
1862	Battles of Velvarde and Glorieta Pass end Confederate occupation of New Mexico.
1862	"Long Walk," in which Navajos and Apaches are relocated to Bosque Redondo. Thousands die of disease and starvation.
1867	Navajos and Apaches allowed to return to their homelands.
1886	Geronimo surrenders and Indian warfare ceases in the Southwest.
1912	New Mexico becomes 47th state.
1916	Pancho Villa raids Columbus, New Mexico.
1917	Mabel Dodge Luhan arrives in New Mexico and settles in Taos.
1920	Women granted right to vote.
1922	D.H. Lawrence arrives in Taos on his 37th birthday. He settles north of Taos on Kiowa Ranch in 1924 and completes the *Plumed Serpent, St. Mawr,* and *The Woman Who Rode Away.*
1927	Willa Cather's *Death Comes for the Archbishop,* a novel about New Mexico, the Catholic Church, and Hispanic life, is published by Alfred A. Knopf.
1929	American icon and artist Georgia O'Keeffe, age 42, arrives in Taos on her first extended visit to New Mexico. She stays with Mabel Dodge Luhan and visits D.H. Lawrence's Kiowa Ranch.
1945	World's first atomic bomb detonated at Trinity Site.
1948	Indians win right to vote in state elections.
1949	Georgia O'Keeffe leaves New York City at age 62 and becomes a permanent resident of the Spanish/Indian Pueblo de Abequ (Abiquiu).
1970	Blue Lake, sacred shrine and place of emergence to Taos Pueblo Indians, is returned to them by the U.S. Government.
2000	President Clinton issues an Executive Order that strengthens his Executive Order of 1998, in which he affirms and protects a tribe's right to self-governance and self-determination, and reiterates that the federal government shall communicate with the tribes as one government to another.

Opposite: Ancient drawings such as these at Petroglyph National Monument in Rinconada Canyon west of Albuquerque date as far back as 3,000 years.

Appendix B

Schedule of Native American Feast Days and Spectacles

*I*f you're planning a trip to New Mexico and want to experience a feast day, use this calendar to see when and where they occur. As with other venues in New Mexico, be sure to call first. Before you attend, read Visiting Sacred Sites on page 19, including How to Behave on page 21. An asterisk in the list indicates events covered in detail in this book or brief listings under the Other Spiritual Events headings.

Jan. 22–23 .... San Ildefonso Feast Day, San Ildefonso, Region Two, 505-455-2273

May 1 .... San Felipe Feast Day, San Felipe, Region Two, 505-867-3381

May 7 .... Santa Maria Feast Day, Acoma, Region One, 800-747-0181

June 13 .... St. Anthony's Feast Day, Sandia, Region Two, 505-867-3317

June 23–24 .... San Juan Feast Day, San Juan, Region Two, 505-852-4400

June 29 .... San Pedro Feast Day, Santa Ana, Region Two, 505-867-3301

July 4 .... *Apache Maidens' Puberty Rites, Mescalero Apache, Region Four, 505-761-4494

July 14 .... San Buenaventura Feast Day, Cochiti, Region Two, 505-465-2244

July 25–26 .... Santa Ana Feast Day, Santa Ana, Region Two, 505-867-3301

Aug. 4 .... *Santo Domingo Feast Day and Green Corn Dance, Santo Domingo, No. 52 in Region Two, 505-465-2214

Aug. 9–10 .... *San Lorenzo Feast Day, Picuris, No. 51 in Region Two, 505-587-2519

Aug. 12 .... Santa Clara Feast Day, Santa Clara, Region Two, 505-753-7326

Aug. 15 .... *Zia Pueblo Feast Day, Zia Pueblo, No. 53 in Region Two, 505-867-3304

Sept. 2 .... San Estevan Feast Day, Acoma, Region One, 505-552-6604

Sept. 4 .... St. Augustine Feast Day, Isleta Pueblo, Region Two, 505-860-3111

Mid-September ... *Go-Jii-Ya Feast Day, Jicarilla Apache, Region One, 505-759-3242

Sept. 19 .... Feast Day of St. Joseph, Laguna Pueblos, Region One, 505-552-6654

Sept. 29–30 .... *San Gerónimo Day, Taos, No. 50 in Region Two, 505-758-9593/1028

Early October ...... *Yei-Be-Chai Healing Ceremony (Nightway Chant), Navajo, Region One, 505-786-5302

Oct. 3–4 .... *Saint Francis of Assisi Feast Day, Nambe, No. 49 in Region Two, 505-455-2036

Nov. 12 .... San Diego Feast Day, Tesuque, Region Two, 505-983-2667; Jemez, Region Two, 505-834-7235

Early December ... *Shalako Dance, Zuni Pueblo, No. 9 in Region One, 505-782-4481

Dec. 11–12 .... Guadalupe Feast Day, Pojoaque, Region Two, 505-455-2278

Dec. 24 .... *Procession of the Virgin, Taos Pueblo, No. 48 in Region Two, 505-758-9593/1028

Opposite: San Miguel Church in Socorro was originally built in 1626.

Appendix C

Retreats by Spiritual Affiliation

Although many spiritual retreats are not affiliated with a specific religion or belief system, some are. If you're looking for a specific type of retreat, use this list. An asterisk in the list indicates a retreat covered in detail in this book; listings without an asterisk appear under the Other Retreats heading that follows the main retreat entries in each region.

Buddhist/Eastern
*Bodhi Manda Zen Center, No. 18 in Region Two
*Hidden Mountain Zen Center, No. 22 in Region Two
*Lama Foundation, (Eastern and Western), No. 24 in Region Two
Sufi Foundation of America, Region Four
*Upaya Zen Center, No. 31 in Region Two
*Vallecitos Mountain Refuge, No. 32 in Region Two

Catholic
*Center for Action and Contemplation, No. 19 in Region Two
*Father Fitzgerald Center, No. 20 in Region Two
*Holy Cross Retreat, No. 76 in Region Five
*La Foresta, No. 23 in Region Two
*Monastery of Christ in the Desert, No. 26 in Region Two
*Our Lady of Guadalupe Benedictine Abbey, No. 28 in Region Two
*Spiritual Renewal Center, No. 30 in Region Two

Protestant
*Black River Center for Learning (Christian), No. 62 in Region Four
*Ghost Ranch (Presbyterian), No. 21 in Region Two
*Mandala Center (Episcopal), No. 56 in Region Three

Non-Affiliated
Casa Blanca B&B, Region Four
Casa de Walela, Region Four
Casa del Gavilan B&B, Region Three
Casa Escondida, Region Two
*Casitas de Gila, No. 75 in Region Five
Corkins Lodge Resort and Wilderness Retreat, Region Two
Heart Seed B&B, Retreat Center, & Spa, Region Two
Inn at the Halona, Region One
Kokopelli's Cave B&B, Region One
Los Olmos Guest Ranch, Region Five
*Mabel Dodge Luhan House Inn and Retreat, No. 25 in Region Two
*Ojo Caliente Mineral Springs Resort, No. 27 in Region Two
*Riverdancer Retreats, No. 29 in Region Two
San Gerónimo Lodge, Region Two
Spirit Ranch Retreat, Region One
Star Hill Inn, Region Three
Taos Art Retreat, Region Two
*Zuni Mountain Lodge, No. 3 in Region One

Opposite: At the Monastery of Christ in the Desert, open to visitors of every spiritual orientation, Benedictine monks live quiet, contemplative lives.

Appendix D

Bibliography and Suggested Reading List

*W*hile learning about New Mexico and writing this book, I consulted many sources. The listings marked with an asterisk are my suggestions for your enlightenment.

Austin, Mary. *Land of Little Rain.* 1903. Reprint. New York: Applewood Books, 1999.*

Baca, Elmo. *Mabel's Santa Fe and Taos.* Salt Lake City: Gibbs Smith, Publisher, 2000.

Cash, Marie Romero. *Living Shrines: Home Altars of New Mexico.* Santa Fe, N.Mex.: Museum of New Mexico Press, 1998.*

Castillo, Ana, ed. *Goddess of the Americas: Writings on the Virgin of Guadalupe.* New York: Riverhead Books, 1996.

Cather, Willa. *Death Comes for the Archbishop.* 1927. Reprint. New York: Vintage Books, 1990.*

deBuys, William. *Enchantment and Exploitation.* Albuquerque, N.Mex.: University of New Mexico Press, 1985.*

———. *River of Traps.* Albuquerque, N.Mex.: University of New Mexico Press, 1990.*

Dunnington, Jacqueline. *Guadalupe: Our Lady of New Mexico.* Santa Fe, N.Mex.: Museum of New Mexico Press, 1999.

———. *Viva Guadalupe!* Santa Fe, N.Mex.: Museum of New Mexico Press, 1997.*

Gandert, Miguel. *Nuevo Mexico Profundo: Rituals of an Indo-Hispano Homeland.* Santa Fe, N.Mex.: Museum of New Mexico Press, 2000.

Horgan, Paul. *Great River: The Rio Grande in North American History.* 2 vols. Minerva Press, 1968.

Julyan, Robert. *The Place Names of New Mexico.* Albuquerque, N.Mex.: University of New Mexico Press, 1998.*

Kutz, Jack. *Mysteries & Miracles of New Mexico.* Corrales, N.Mex.: Rhombus Publishing Co., 1988.*

Lawrence, D.H. *The Plumed Serpent.* 1926. Reprint. New York: Wordsworth Editions, 1999.*

———. *The Woman Who Rode Away and Other Classics.* New York: Penguin, 1997.*

Locke, Raymond. *The Book of the Navajo.* Los Angeles: Mankind Publishing, 1992.

Luhan, Mabel Dodge. *The Edge of Taos Desert.* Albuquerque, N.Mex.: University of New Mexico Press, 1987.*

MacMahon, James. *Deserts*. Audubon Society Nature Guides. New York: Alfred A.Knopf, 1985.

McLuhan, T.C. *Dream Tracks: The Railroad and the American Indian 1890–1930*. Harry Abrams, Inc., 1985.

Momaday, N. Scott. *House Made of Dawn*. New York: Harper & Row, 1968.*

Nealson, Christina. *Living on the Spine: A Woman's Life in the Sangre de Cristo Mountains*. 1997. Reprint. Englewood, Colo: Westcliffe Publishers, 2001.

Nichols, John. *On the Mesa*. New York: Ancient City Press, 1995.*

———. *The Last Beautiful Days of Autumn*. New York: Holt, Rinehart and Winston, 1982.*

———. *The Milagro Beanfield War*. New York: Ballantine Books, 1974.*

Noble, David. *Pueblos, Villages, Forts & Trails: A Guide to New Mexico's Past*. Albuquerque, N.Mex.: University of New Mexico Press, 1994.

Ortiz, Alfonso. *The Tewa World*. Chicago: University of Chicago Press, 1969.

Parent, Laurence. *Hiking New Mexico*. Helena, Mont.: Falcon Press, 1998.*

Pearce, T.M. *New Mexico Place Names*. Albuquerque, N.Mex.: University of New Mexico Press, 1965.

Pratt, Boyd C. *Gone But Not Forgotten*. 2 vols. Santa Fe, N.Mex.: Historic Preservation Division, New Mexico Office of Cultural Affairs, 1986.

Sagar, Keith. *D.H. Lawrence and New Mexico*. Salt Lake City: Gibbs Smith, Publisher, 1982.*

Sagel, Jim. *El Santo Queso/The Holy Cheese*. Albuquerque, N.Mex.: University of New Mexico Press, 1996.*

Sherman, John. *Taos: A Pictorial History*. Santa Fe, N.Mex.: William Gannon, 1990.

Silko, Leslie Marmon. *Ceremony*. New York: Penguin Books, 1988.*

Staats, Todd. *Off the Beaten Path*. Guilford, Conn.: Globe Pequot Press, 2000.*

Steele, Thomas J. *Santos and Saints: The Religious Folk Art of Hispanic New Mexico*. Santa Fe, N.Mex.: Ancient City Press, 1994.

Sze, Corinne. "La Capilla de San Ysidro Labrador." Santa Fe, N.Mex.: Historic Santa Fe Foundation, March 26, 1998.

Tyler, Hamilton. *Pueblo Birds & Myths*. Flagstaff, Ariz.: Northland Publishing, 1991.

Wallis, Michael, and Craig Varjabedian. *En Divina Luz: Penitente Moradas of New Mexico*. Albuquerque, N.Mex.: University of New Mexico Press, 1994.*

Walker, Barbara G. *The Woman's Dictionary of Symbols and Sacred Objects*. San Francisco: HarperSanFrancisco, 1988.

Index

NOTE: Citations followed by the letter "p" denote photos; citations followed by the letter "m" denote maps.

Abiquiu, 86–87, 98–99, 115–117

Alamogordo, 188–191

Albuquerque, 82–83, 88–89, 106–109, 118–119, 128–130, 135–137, 147–148, 206–207

Alkali Flat Trail, White Sands National Monument, 172m, 190–191, 190p

Angel Fire, 78–79

Artesia, 174–175

Aztec, 36–38

Aztec Ruins, The Great Kiva, 34m, 36–38, 36p

Aztec Ruins National Monument, 36–38

Bandelier National Monument, 122–124, 141–144

Black River, 179–180

Black River Center for Learning, 172m, 179–180, 179p

Bodhi Manda Zen Center, 58m, 80–81, 80p

Bosque del Apache National Wildlife Refuge, 236–237

bultos, definition of, 25

Caballo Resource Area, 188–189

Cambalache, 58m, 145

Capulin, 164–165

Capulin Volcano National Monument, 158m, 164–165, 164p

Carlsbad, 179–180, 183–187

Carlsbad Bat Flights, Mass Ascension, 172m, 192–193, 192p

Carlsbad Caverns National Park, 183–184, 192–193

Carrizozo, 176–178

Casitas de Gila, 200m, 210–211, 210p

Castle Springs Creek, 179–180

Catwalk, The, 200m, 214–215, 214p

cave, definition of, 25

Cebolleta, 39–41

Center for Action and Contemplation, Tepeyac Guest House, 58m, 82–83, 82p

Cerro Pedernal (Flint Peak), 58m, 115–117, 115p

Chaco Canyon, Supernova Pictograph, 34m, 44–47, 44p, 46p

Chaco Culture National Historical Park, 44–47

Chama, 98–99, 125–127

Chimayo, 61–63

Clayton, 169–170

Cliff, 220–221

Cochiti Pueblo, 128–130

Columbus, 202–203, 229–231

confluence (river), definition of, 25

Corrales, 118–119

Corrales Bosque Preserve, 58m, 118–119, 118p

cristo, definition of, 25

Crownpoint, 44–47

crucifix, definition of, 25

Cuba, 90–92

Datil, 216–217

Datil Well National Recreation Area, 216–217

Datil Well Woodlands, 200m, 216–217, 216p

Deming, 229–231

descanso, definition of, 25

Des Moines, 162–163

D.H. Lawrence Memorial, 58m, 120–121, 121p

Dia de los Muertos Celebration, Calavera Coalition, 200m, 234–236, 234p

Dineh, definition of, 26

Douglas fir, definition of, 26

Dripping Springs Natural Area, 224–226

Dwan Light Sanctuary, 158m, 160–161, 160p

El Camino Real, definition of, 26

El Malpais National Monument, Sandstone Bluffs Overlook, 34m, 48–49, 48p

El Morro National Monument, 34m, 50–51, 50p

El Santuario de Chimayo, 58m, 61–63, 61p

Española, 100–102

farolitos, definition of, 26
Father Fitzgerald Center, 58m, 84–85, 84p
Flint Peak (Cerro Pedernal), 58m, 115–117, 115p
fountains, definition of, 31
Frijoles Canyon, 58m, 122–124, 122p

Gallup, 42–43
geoglyphs, definition of, 26
Ghost Ranch, 58m, 86–87, 86p
Gila, 210–211
Gila Cliff Dwellings, 200m, 218–219, 218p
Gila Cliff Dwellings National Monument, 218–219
Gila Riparian Reserve, 200m, 220–221, 220p
Gila River Valley, 220–221
Glenwood, 214–215
Gran Quivira Ruins, 172m, 181–182, 181p
Grants, 48–51, 54–55
Great Kiva, Aztec Ruins, 34m, 36–38, 36p

Hanover, 208–209, 222–223
Hermit Peak, 158m, 166–168, 166p
Heron Lake, 58m, 125–127, 126p
Heron Lake State Park, 125–127
Hidden Mountain Zen Center, 58m, 88–89, 88p
hills, definition of, 26
Holloman AFB, 190–191
Holy Cross Retreat, 200m, 212–213, 212p
Hot-Air Balloon Fiesta, Mass Ascension, 58m, 147–148, 147p

ions, definition of, 26
Islamic Musalla, 58m, 64–65, 64p

Jemez Springs, 80–81, 84–85, 106–107

Kasha-Katuwe Tent Rocks National Monument, 58m, 128–130, 128p
Kiowa National Grassland, 169–170
Kit Carson Memorial Park Cemetery, 58m, 131–132, 131p

kiva, definition of, 27
Kneeling Nun Mountain, 200m, 222–223, 222p

labyrinth, definition of, 27
La Capilla de San Ysidro Labrador, 58m, 66–67, 66p
La Conquistadora Chapel and Shrine, 58m, 68–70, 68p
La Cueva, 200m, 224–226, 224p
Lady on the Mountain, 200m, 227–228, 227p
La Foresta, 58m, 90–92, 90p
Laguna Pueblo, 39–41
La Jara, 90–92
lake, definition of, 27
Lake Arthur, 174–175
Lama Foundation, 58m, 93–94, 93p
Las Cruces, 188–189, 212–213, 224–226
Las Posadas, 58m, 146
Las Vegas, 160–161, 166–168
La Vista Verde Trail, Rio Grande Gorge, 58m, 133–134, 133p
Lincoln National Forest, 185–187
Loretto Chapel Miraculous Staircase, 58m, 71–73, 71p
Los Alamos, 122–124, 141–144
Los Ojos, 125–127
Los Portales Shrine, 34m, 39–41, 39p
luminarias, definition of, 27

Mabel Dodge Luhan House Inn and Retreat, 58m, 95–97, 96p
Magdalena, 227–228, 232–233
Magdalena Mountain, 227–228
Mandala Center, 158m, 162–163, 162p
Manzano Hawk Watch, Mass Migration of Raptors, 172m, 193–195, 194p
Manzano Mountains State Park, 193–195
maps
    North Central New Mexico, 58m
    Northeast New Mexico, 158m
    Northwest New Mexico, 34m
    Regions of New Mexico, 8m–9m
    Southeast New Mexico, 172m
    Southwest New Mexico, 200m
Marian shrine, definition of, 27

Mass Ascension, Carlsbad Bat Flights, 172m, 192–193, 192p
Mass Ascension, Hot-Air Balloon Fiesta, 58m, 147–148, 147p
Mass Ascension, Water Birds, 200m, 236–237, 237p
Mass Migration of Raptors, Manzano Hawk Watch, 172m, 193–195, 194p
Mesilla, 234–236
Mesilla Park, 212–213
Mills Canyon, 158m, 169–170, 169p
miracle, definition of, 27
Miraculous Tortilla Shrine, 172m, 174–175, 174p
monastery, definition of, 27
Monastery of Christ in the Desert, 58m, 98–99, 98p
Montezuma, 160–161
morada, definition of, 27
mountain, definition of, 28
Mountainair, 181–182
mountaintop, definition of, 28
Mt. Taylor Ranger District, 54–55

Nageezi, 44–47
Nambe Pueblo, 150
National Radio Astronomy Observatory, 232–233

Ojo Caliente, 100–102
Ojo Caliente Mineral Springs Resort, 58m, 100–102, 100p
Organ Mountains, 224–226
Orilla Verde Recreation Area, 133–134
Our Lady of Guadalupe Benedictine Abbey, 58m, 103–105, 104p
Our Lady of Guadalupe Church, 200m, 202–203, 202p

Palomas, Mexico, 202–203
Pancho Villa Memorial, 200m, 229–231, 229p
Pancho Villa State Park, 229–231
Pecos, 103–105
Penitentes, Brotherhood of, definition of, 28
petroglyph, definition of, 29
Petroglyph National Monument, Rinconada Canyon, 58m, 135–137, 136p

pictograph, definition of, 29
Picuris Pueblo, 153
Pilar, 133–134
Pilgrimage in Honor of La Virgen de Guadalupe, 200m, 238–240
piñon pine, definition of, 29
plaza, definition of, 29
Procession of the Virgin, 58m, 149
pueblo etiquette, definition of, 30
Pueblo Revolt of 1680, 30
pueblos, definition of, 30

Questa, 145

Ramah, 50–51
Ranchos de Taos, 74–75, 146
Raton, 162–165
Rattlesnake Springs, 172m, 183–184, 183p
reredos, definition of, 30
retablo, definition of, 30
retreat, definition of, 15, 30
Rinconada Canyon, Petroglyph National Monument, 58m, 135–137, 136p
Rio Grande Gorge, La Vista Verde Trail, 58m, 133–134, 133p
Rio Grande River, 118–119, 133–134
Rio Pueblo River, 133–134
river, definition of, 30–31
Riverdancer Retreats, 58m, 106–107, 106p
rock, definition of, 31
Rock with Wings (Tsé Bit' A'i), 34m, 52–53, 52p
Roswell, 174–175
Roy, 169–170
ruins, definition of, 31

sacred places, definition of, 15
Saint Francis of Assisi Feast Day, 58m, 150
Salinas Pueblo Missions National Monument, 181–182
San Agustin, Plains of, 232–233
San Antonio, 236–237
San Antonio Mountain, 58m, 138–140, 138p
San Cristobal, 93–94, 120–121
sanctuaries, definition of, 15

Sandia Pueblo, 118–119

Sandstone Bluffs Overlook, El Malpais National Monument, 34m, 48–49, 48p

San Francisco de Asis Church, 58m, 74–75, 74p

San Gerónimo Day, 58m, 151–152

Sangre de Cristo Mountains, 93–94, 120–121

San Lorenzo, 204–205

San Lorenzo Feast Day, 58m, 153

San Lorenzo Mission, 200m, 204–205, 204p

San Mateo Mountains, 54–55

San Miguel Church, 200m, 206–207, 206p

Santa Fe, 61–63, 66–73, 76–77, 98–99, 103–105, 110–111, 122–124, 128–130, 141–142, 156

Santa Fe National Forest, 115–117

Santa Rita Shrine, 200m, 208–209, 208p

santo, definition of, 31

Santo Domingo Feast Day and Green Corn Dance, 58m, 154

Santo Domingo Pueblo, 154

Santo Niño de Atocha Chapel, 172m, 176–178, 176p

Santuario de Nuestra Señora de Guadalupe, 58m, 76–77, 76p

Seboyeta, 39–41

Shalako Dance, 34m, 56

Shiprock Pinnacle, 52–53

shrine, definition of, 31

Shrine of the Stone Lions, 58m, 141–142, 141p

Silver City, 204–205, 208–209, 214–215, 218–223

Sitting Bull Falls, 172m, 185–187, 186p

Socorro, 206–207, 216–217, 232–233

spiritual events, definition of, 15

Spiritual Renewal Center, 58m, 108–109, 108p

springs, definition of, 31

St. Francis of Assisi Cathedral, 68–70

Supernova Pictograph, Chaco Canyon, 34m, 44–47, 44p, 46p

Taos, 64–65, 74–75, 78–79, 93–97, 112–114, 120–121, 131–134

Taos Pueblo, 149, 151–152

Taylor, Mt. (Tsoodzil), 34m, 54–55, 54p

Tepeyac Guest House, Center for Action and Contemplation, 58m, 82–83, 82p

Tewas, definition of, 31

Thoreau, 42–43

Three Rivers, 176–178

Three Rivers Petroglyph Site, 172m, 188–189, 188p

Tiwas (Northern and Southern), definition of, 31

Tortugas, 238–240

Towas, definition of, 31

tree, definition of, 31–32

Tres Piedras, 138–140

Trinity Site, 172m, 195–198, 197p

Tsankawi Indian Ruins, 58m, 143–144, 143p

Tsé Bit' A'i (Rock with Wings), 34m, 52–53, 52p

Tsoodzil (Mt. Taylor), 34m, 54–55, 54p

Tularosa, 176–178

Upaya Zen Center, 58m, 110–111, 110p

Vallecitos Mountain Refuge, 58m, 112–114, 112p

Very Large Array (VLA), 200m, 232–233, 232p

Vietnam Veterans National Memorial Chapel of Peace and Brotherhood, 58m, 78–79, 78p

volcano, definition of, 32

water, definition of, 32

Water Birds, Mass Ascension, 200m, 236–237, 237p

waterfall, definition of, 32

well, definition of, 31

White Sands Missile Range, 195–198

White Sands National Monument, Alkali Flat Trail, 172m, 190–191, 190p

Youngsville, 115–117

Zia Pueblo, 155

Zia Pueblo Feast Day, 58m, 155

Zozobra, 58m, 156

Zuni Mountain Lodge, 34m, 42–43, 42p

Zuni Pueblo, 56

About the Author/Photographer

Christina Nealson, born and raised in the Iowa heartland, has lived in the Southwest—including Colorado, Arizona, and New Mexico—for 25 years. Her travels have taken her across the United States and into Canada, Mexico, Central America, Europe, and Africa. Nealson's essays appear frequently in various regional magazines, major western newspapers, and books, including *Writers on the Range* (University Press of Colorado, 1998) and *Living in the Runaway West* (Fulcrum Publishing, 2000). A contributing editor of *Horse Fly,* a monthly journal of news and culture in Taos, N.M., Nealson is also the author of *At the Edge: Cooperative Teachings for Global Survival* and *Living on the Spine: A Woman's Life in the Sangre de Cristo Mountains.*

Nealson's current projects include a novel, nonfiction book *Menopause, Nature and the Unlived Soul,* and a compilation of essays on life in the Southwest.

Nealson has been a psychotherapist since 1977, and the mother of her precious daughter, Hope, since 1970. She lives and writes in Taos with her husband, writer Tom Wolf, a big black dog, and three cats.

For further information on Nealson's life, writing and photography, visit her website at http://www.christinanealson.com.

Photo by Tom Wolf